Democracy Begins Bet

Democracy Begins Between Two

LUCE IRIGARAY

Translated by KIRSTEEN ANDERSON

THE ATHLONE PRESS
LONDON

First published in 2000 by
THE ATHLONE PRESS
1 Park Drive, London NW 11 7SG

This English Translation © The Athlone Press 2000

Originally published as *La democrazia comincia a due*
© Bollati Boringhieri 1994

British Library Cataloguing in Publication Data
*A catalogue record for this book is available
from the British Library*

ISBN 0 485 11503 4 HB
0 485 12123 9 PB

All rights reserved. No part of this publication may be reproduced, stored in a retrieval system, or transmitted in any form or by any means, electronic, mechanical, photocopying or otherwise, without prior permission in writing from the publisher.

Typeset by CentraServe, Saffron Walden, Essex
Printed and bound in Great Britain by
MPG Books Ltd, Bodmin, Cornwall

Contents

Translator's Note   vii
List of Acronyms   xi

Introduction   1
I Want Love, Not War   21
Feminine Identity: Biology or Social Conditioning?   30
Women's Enslavement   40
How To Manage the Transition from Natural to Civil Coexistence?   49
Towards a Citizenship of the European Union   60
Refounding the Family on a Civil Basis   95
Democracy is Love   106
The Question of the Other   121
A Two-Subject Culture   142
Ten Suggestions for the Construction of the European Union   156

Democracy Begins Between Two

Politics and Happiness	165
The Representation of Women	174
Europe Captivated by New Myths	185
Appendix	191
Notes	216
Index	217

Translator's Note

Irigaray's main concern in *Democracy Begins Between Two* is the need for Western culture to grant full recognition to the two genders, female and male, which make up our society. In translating from Italian into English, grammatical gender is obviously an important issue. Since Italian marks all its nouns and adjectives as masculine or feminine, where English does not, a translator must find a way of making sure that this gender marking, if relevant to the meaning of the text, is transferred into the translated version. I will mention the main features of the translation which are at stake here.

'Al femminile', 'al maschile', rather elliptical in the Italian, have been translated as 'in female/male mode' meaning, in a style or form or mode appropriate to the gender in question. Italian does not distinguish between 'male' and 'masculine' or 'female' and 'feminine'; both meanings are covered by 'maschile' or 'femminile'. So, although I tend to use 'masculine' and 'feminine', terms normally assumed to refer to the cultural level, the

vii

Democracy Begins Between Two

biological connotations of 'male' and 'female' are not excluded.

Irigaray, whose initial research was psycholinguistic, is greatly interested in how the play of power between the genders affects, and is affected, by linguistic structures and usage. She experiments with words textually, in their physical form, to draw attention to their potential to bear more than one meaning or to reveal their syntactic and semantic biases. I have tried to reproduce this play with word forms in the target text: 'uomo(ini)', embracing singular and plural forms, translates as 'ma(e)n', 'donna(e)' as 'woma(e)n'. For adjectives and nouns, where the Italian neatly telescopes the two genders by bracketing the feminine ending after the masculine – 'altro(a)', 'other', an adjective in the singular, or 'cittadini(e)', 'citizens', a noun in the plural – I have tended to translate with the insertion of 'male and female' as in 'the other, male and female' or 'male and female citizens'. As far as personal pronouns are concerned, the combined form 's/he' is used where appropriate. Similar combined forms are 'each wo/man' and 'all wo/men', which echo the Italian pronouns 'ciascuna(o)', 'each', in the singular, and 'tutte(i)', 'all', in the plural, which position the feminine form before the bracketed masculine form.

Where Italian uses a possessive adjective in the masculine to refer to either gender as in 'suo' ('one's'), I have usually translated with the combined form 'his/

Translator's Note

her'. This is a little unwieldy, but has the advantage of maintaining the distinction between the genders in textual form.

Aside from questions of gender, the most tricky translation point involves 'due'. This occurs in various formulations – 'due, a due, in due ' – as, for example, in the Italian title *La Democrazia comincia a due*. The concept at issue here, that of acting or thinking or operating as two distinct subjectivities, as two different genders, is fundamental to Irigaray's argument but unfortunately lacks a neat equivalent in English. It derives from the French 'deux', as in 'un dîner à deux', in which two individuals participate, but this is not, in fact, natural in Italian idiom either. I have translated it variously, depending on context, as 'two', 'being-two', 'as two beings' and, occasionally, 'between two'. If it sounds a little strange in English, it is also a little odd in Italian. The point here is that Irigaray is deliberately stretching language to make it say new things.

Another important recurrent term is 'la convivenza', used mainly in the formulation 'la convivenza civile', meaning 'living alongside each other in civil society'. Since this is rather cumbersome in English, I translate 'convivenza' as 'coexistence' as in 'la convivenza civile', 'civil coexistence' or 'la convivenza comunitaria', 'coexistence in the community'. As far as I know, this use of 'convivenza/coexistence' has no philosophical overtones of, say, Heideggerian *mitsein* or of a phenomenological nature. Irigaray seems to be using it to refer to how we manage our lives together in contemporary society, given the range of races, ages, cultures and life-styles which inevitably rub shoulders in Western Europe. 'Civile', it should be noted, means both 'civil' and 'civilized' in Italian. I retained 'civil', on the whole, as in 'in a civil manner' ('in un modo civile') or 'civil life' ('la vita civile'), since the shorter form necessarily implies the longer: one is civil, capable of living in civil society, because one has been civilized. Clearly, 'civile' has links with 'civismo' or 'public-spiritedness' and can also connote secular, as opposed to ecclesiastical, life.

Two final points. I translate 'persona', meaning 'person' or 'individual', as 'individual'; this seems to me to read better in most of the contexts in which it is used. Similarly, 'singolarità', 'singularity' or 'uniqueness', is consistently rendered as 'singularity'.

Square brackets [. . .] indicate translator's additions.

Kirsteen Anderson
London

List of Acronyms

CNRS   Centre National de la Recherche Scientifique
       National Centre for Scientific Research, Paris
FGCI   Federazione Giovanile Comunista Italiana
       Federation of Young Italian Communists
PCI   Partito Comunista Italiano
       Italian Communist Party
PDS   Partito di Democrazia Socialista
       Social Democratic Party
ONISEP Office National d'Information sur les
       Enseignements et les Professions
       National Office for Information on
       Educational and Professional Training, Paris

Introduction

The aim of this book is to initiate a working collaboration with the Commission for Equal Opportunities for men and women in the region of Emilia-Romagna, which invited me to act as adviser in promoting a training in citizenship, both for adults and children, at the regional and European levels.

Contrary to the tendency of our times, which encourages one to act first then see what happens, Paola Bottoni, who heads the Commission, wanted some form of theoretical work to be the prompting inspiration behind the decisions and the way things were to be carried out.

A decision of this sort shows a deep understanding of women's tradition where knowledge, and sometimes the book, is transmitted from mother to daughter. Making equal opportunities for women possible does not mean that women should simply model themselves on masculine ways of being and doing, but that they should enjoy equivalent opportunities to men in all aspects of life and particularly in the sphere of education. So it is a question of discovering what woman is and what she wants; and of opening up ways for

Democracy Begins Between Two

her to bring her identity and her subjectivity into being.

Paola Bottoni's request is, moreover, pleasing to me, as a Frenchwoman, because it allows me to remain loyal to certain masters of the Italian Left – Antonio Gramsci and Enrico Berlinguer, to mention only two of them – for whom political coexistence can only operate if it is in conjunction with thought and, indeed, poetry. In their view, it must also be based on teaching, if democracy is to be real rather than formal or totalizing; and if culture is to be the means by which each man and woman is helped to acquire an equal human dignity and to determine him/herself politically with awareness and in freedom, without having to give up his/her own, say religious, opinions.

Thanks to these qualities, Italian communism has never been like other forms of communism and, through both the heart and the head, has contributed to enriching civilization in ways that deserve to be remembered and developed. We are talking here about an inheritance that has universal value and which involves people belonging to different political and cultural horizons. Personally speaking, in the name of the liberation of woma(e)n, I have avoided any party allegiance but I cannot deny that I have learnt lessons from the Italian Left which I do not wish to forget. This does not mean that I toe the line in every respect, but that I want to engage in a dialogue and come face to face with the people who genuinely respect such a tradition for the value it attributes, for example, to a secularity

Introduction

defined positively rather than simply in opposition to religion.

But History does not cease to unfold, so that remaining faithful to a tradition means conserving its spirit while nonetheless making it relevant to the circumstances of a different era.

Amongst these, some appear today more crucial than others:

1. The liberation of women from subjection to a natural function: that of being the one who is used for love-making, for giving birth, for providing nourishment without enjoying an identity and a dignity of her own in private or public life.
2. The discovery of cultures that are different from those of the Western subject, cultures with which this subject must now coexist, whether on national territory or beyond its borders; cultures which call into question the self-consciousness of this subject as a universally valid model.
3. The opening-up of national boundaries in favour of coalitions or voluntary groupings of peoples for military, economic and cultural purposes, the European Union being the most recent example.
4. The fact that the planet Earth is threatened by various forms of exploitation and pollution, and that human consciousness is, in a different way, as a result of the extension of technologies which disturb the relation to the self and relationships with others. These dimensions of the spirit are themselves in

difficulty because of the excessively mobile nature of our culture.

The present state of human, and particularly Western, industrial civilization, creates, then, problems concerning not only the exploitation of one social class by another or of a poor country by a wealthy one, but also the exploitation of the human species and the space in which it lives. Deciding what is to be done is no longer simply a question of defining the right salary for a certain job, or of knowing how to help the less industrialized nations to develop, nor even of how to create jobs to absorb unemployment. It is much more a case of reorganizing the way that humanity lives and produces with a view to preserving the planet, and human life and culture. In other words, of awakening consciousness to another stage in its becoming, which will allow us to begin building new ways of existing and thinking.

If we are to avoid being simply impotent survivors or regressing to a basic human identity which knows nothing but the level of need – food, clothing, a roof over our head, etc. – and of the instincts – communication, emotion, sex, – we have to take a step forward in human becoming. The new circumstances of the present era moreover encourage, and indeed oblige us, to do so.

If man's dealings with woman are to be equal, he will have to face a culture of sexual desire and of

Introduction

coexistence in difference of which he, as yet, knows nothing. This requires a reorganization of the relationship between sensibility and intellect, between body or emotions and civil existence. It is also a question of rethinking love and of refounding the family.

The family is, in any event, in crisis, is changing, as a result of the coexistence within it of various traditions, of various customary laws, which are forcing it to reassess what was previously taken for granted: love, relationships.

A 'marriage' between a white (male or female) and a black (male or female), a Christian (male or female) and a Moslem (male or female) cannot possibly adhere to the same customs or the same laws as a 'marriage' between a white Catholic man and woman. Belonging to a different class is no longer the main obstacle preventing people getting married – many others now exist! These new difficulties, which men and women who love each other have to resolve, are concrete proof that we have now entered a new era in History for which the already existing institutions are no longer adequate.

This is true of the family in the narrow sense of the term, but it is also true of all the types of family which have contributed to the structuring of society along with it, in other words, political, cultural and religious families, etc. Coexistence between genders, between races, between generations, but also between religions, cultures, political parties or regimes, compels us to interpret what used to constitute the parameters within which we moved with no awareness of the laws governing them.

We must now change the context in which we live and, more radically, the framework of our identity. This entails a revolution as wide, if not far more wide-ranging, than the Copernican one.

We have to rethink the model of subjectivity which has served us for centuries, not in order to add a little bit here or a little bit there, but so that we can abandon the model of a single and singular subject altogether. This does not mean that the one of the subject can become many (plus one or minus one), but that the subject is at least two, man and woman, a two in relations that are not biunivocal.

The Western subject has, then, lost its horizon and, in a more general sense, a horizon, a homeland and a consciousness which were obedient to its laws. Yet it is not, for all that, submissive to a God of the same gender, of which it is simply an imperfect image; rather, it has come to be limited and defined by an other which is irreducible to it: the other gender. And it is similarly determined by other cultures. But the difference between the genders appears, not at first sight perhaps but after some reflection, as the most radical limit opposed to the totalizing will of the subject. In fact, it is more universal than any other and implies, in addition, that there is, for each gender, a relation between nature and culture that is specific to it. If some

Introduction

cultures appear to us as more foreign than the other gender, this is because we have not yet experienced the distancing that lies in what is closest to us. We become merged with the man or the woman that we embrace, with whom we share our bed, a home, lunch or work. We make him/her ours to escape the insurmountable difference that separates us. We can try to understand another culture because it can be viewed as the outcome of a development in time; but the other, if s/he is still alive, remains incomprehensible to us since, with every moment, s/he is the source of new gestures whose origin remains a mystery to us. The other is moving within a horizon, and constructing a world, that lie beyond us. If we believe that we can make them ours, we are sacrificing both ourselves and the other (male or female) to an illusory desire for possession.

Renouncing the desire to possess the other, in order to recognize him as other, is perhaps the most useful and the most beautiful of the tasks which fall to us. It allows us to move into a new stage in the History of the relation between the genders but also of that between races, generations, traditions.

It also leads to a respect for nature through the other, insofar as this other represents a nature and a culture distinct from my own, from ours.

The human ideal has, for centuries, been associated with the capacity to dominate, to tame, to produce and encourage production with one's own instruments and methods, to cultivate – nature, the other, others – for oneself. Yet, if the human species is to have a future, the ideal should assert itself as a willingness to respect nature, the other, others.

A training in citizenship is thus a priority if we are to make this new historical horizon a reality; a training in respect for oneself but also in respect for the environment, for the other and for others, both alike, and different from us.

Respect for others' property and for the national heritage is no longer sufficient as a gauge of attainment in civil life, unless everything is to be reduced to property: body, culture, religion, race, age, love, sex, etc. Of course, our civil codes have accustomed us to evaluate almost everything in terms of property including, for the most part, conjugal and parental love, community feeling. Yet legislation of this kind has not so far managed to avoid, or to arbitrate in, the conflicts between the sexes, between generations and citizens. As well as war in the strict sense, war between nations, for example, civil society is torn by many forms of violence which the recourse to penal law sanctions from time to time without addressing the causes which are, more often than not, linked with the ownership of property.

To deal with these forms of violence, taking into account the new circumstances which characterize our era, it is necessary to define civil rights relating to individuals and to the relations between them, and not only relating to the ownership of goods.

*

Introduction

If we take respect for the individual as such, with his/her qualities and differences, as our starting point, it is possible to define a form of citizenship appropriate to the necessities of our age: coexistence of the sexes, of generations, races and traditions.

Education for civil life becomes an education in being, rather than in having: being oneself, being with others, male and female, being in and with nature, being in a moment of History, etc. The development of certain values is indispensable for this new form of citizenship: values of communication, not only in the sense of the transmission of information but as communication-between. Relations between individuals are thus prioritized, with respect for things and possessions following as a consequence.

Language therefore assumes a greater importance, and it becomes essential to discover universal modalities which do not sacrifice the singular and the particular detail to neutral, abstract and, in a sense, dead codes. From this point of view, taking the sexed characteristics of language and of discourse into consideration appears as a crucial step towards safeguarding the universal relation between two singularities, as is that between man and woman.

But perhaps a sexually-marked civil code is the minimal guarantee needed to protect the singularity of man, that of woman, and the relation between them. If only we had an alphabet capable of universality that did not destroy human qualities. The objection, in this instance, that the sexes are treated differently in different traditions does not hold up. It is precisely coexistence between traditions that civil codes must guarantee, leaving each man and woman free to make the more ideological choices.

Enrico Berlinguer's teaching on the subject of the separation of Catholic ideology and political secularity could be applied to sexist ideology. Only a society which guarantees civil relations between ma(e)n and woma(e)n, and which leaves the other subjective choices to the individual, can be considered secular.

In this way, universal values lose their rigid and normative character. All that exists is a framework protecting relations between individuals, within which specific qualities play a part so long as civil coexistence is guaranteed. The relationship is primordial, and training in citizenship is concerned with relationship rather than ownership.

Yet letting go of an imperialist ego is not enough to ensure relationship. We have to define objective methods of guaranteeing rights and duties for different subjectivities. From this there follows the necessity of universal civil rights – at least within a given community – which will organize coexistence in a secular context. In fact, if each man and woman asserts: 'This is my right', without a code to limit a subjective claim of this sort, his/her words are no different from a declaration of war. Any man or woman can try shouting louder: 'It's my right'. But what will resolve this? Is

Introduction

it only the penal code that is to sanction claims that overstep the limits?

The assertion: 'This corresponds to my right' should be established by a written text to which reference can be made in case of controversy, and even before it is challenged, by way of norms which do not automatically concede that might is right. Such norms should not only regulate relationships with possessions, but also relationships between individuals. The divisions which at present run through the civil community require us to redefine positively the rights of each man and woman with the aim of making possible a democracy between genders, generations, races, traditions, cultures, etc.

The necessity of sexed rights thus belongs within the wider sphere of juridical reform. Situating it in reality in this way does not make it less urgent, but, on the contrary, helps to clarify its meaning thanks to a wider context of human liberation.

Moreover, rights to protect the identity of women would offer a means of defining a level of equality between women without diminishing their diversity. Insofar as they are citizens, women are in some sense equivalent, and this in no way deprives them of their own qualities. Their dignity is also the equal of men's in spite of the fact that women and men observe customs as, also, rules and rights that are, in certain respects, distinct.

Solving the problem of civil coexistence between the

sexes and the genders seems the most complex way of organizing coexistence between different identities within the horizon of an equality of rights.

Sexual difference is perhaps the hardest way, but it is also the key, to achieving civil coexistence between other forms of difference. An apprenticeship in respect for the other at the most instinctive, emotional level, leads to peaceful coexistence with all forms of otherness.

Recognizing that the other – man or woman – is different from me, and accepting that his/her right to exist and to human dignity is equivalent to mine, leads to the recognition of other forms of diversity. It also forces us to understand that the codes governing civil coexistence have to be, in part, rewritten, if we are to arrive at a genuinely secular level of citizenship.

This goal serves as one of the threads connecting the texts which follow. Whether the discussion concerns the definition of national or supranational citizenship, of civil coexistence in France, Italy or Europe, the objective remains: that of knowing how to ensure respect for differences in the context of equivalent dignity and rights for each of us, male and female. This task seems typical of our era. It is becoming a priority everywhere and, in refusing the challenge, we run the risk of conflict, war and regression in human civilization.

But difference is not limited to the form in which it has already emerged, one that is artificially constructed, as, for example, that which separated the Eastern and

Introduction

Western blocks in the shape of the Berlin Wall. Difference is present everywhere, in us and between us. This gap has to be considered now on pain of political or cultural collapse, or of the constitution of entities or identities that are more dangerous than in the past: new ethnic entities and identities, for example. We have to move beyond allowing difference to give rise to factions and coalitions which in turn may be the source of war and conflicts.

Difference must become an everyday concern in every encounter between two individuals. From this point of view, the difference between ma(e)n and woma(e)n appears a possible model for a new era in History. Respect for the other exists here with the greatest degree of proximity, in the relationship between nature and culture, in the intimacy of the home yet also in civil life. An ethic of sexual difference could, if practised with those closest to us as well as those furthest away, modify our culture: our way of thinking as much as our way of behaving politically.

In place of an era of domination, production, exploitation, there could come into being an era of coexistence, awareness of limits, and respect for natural and cultural riches. We would thus, from historical necessity, enter another stage in the process of human becoming.

As far as the ground which I have covered goes, women's liberation was the first goal to be attained. I tried to achieve it through my critique of Western, mono-subjective culture, my work on the constitution of the feminine subject, my work on the recognition by the feminine subject of the alterity of masculine identity. The aim of women's liberation seems to me to belong now within a wider context which recognizes similar kinds of requirement. Working on European citizenship, I can see that the demand for women's rights is part of a vaster whole where the right to difference has become incontrovertible. It is not only a question of the right to be different-from, since this risks giving rise to further conflicts between entities and blocks, but of the right and the duty to be diverse-between. Thus, not: 'I'm different from you', but: 'we differ amongst ourselves', which implies a continual give-and-take in the establishing of boundaries and relationships, without the one having greater authority over the other.

In this respect, I also felt that women's liberation should come about through a dialectic with the other gender and its liberation.

This is essential not only at the general cultural level, but also at the more restricted level of civil coexistence. Unless the affirmation of my subjectivity occurs in a dialectical process with the other gender, it often becomes nothing but the feminine gender's claim to a self-affirmation [positività] that is as ingenuous as it is conflict-ridden: I, woman, am everywhere and always the best, and achieving my affirmation as woman is the most important accomplishment that I can offer to humanity.

*

Introduction

Of course, I have no desire to deny either the importance or the difficulty of such an accomplishment, but it seems to me impossible to claim to be a fully-realized woman unless one has come to an awareness of oneself as both a subjective and an objective part of the human species. Nor is it enough to state this in an abstract way. We have to try to define the characteristics of both these parts.

This objective has led me, along with other researchers or research groups, to conduct research into the way that men and women speak. I, we, have thus discovered that language, as, too, the ways in which worlds or communities are constituted, possesses features that are specific to men or women, that is, to each sex, to each gender. Women, in fact, privilege intersubjectivity, relationship with the other gender, the relationship of being-two, the physical and, particularly, natural environment, the present and future tenses. Men, in contrast, prefer the subject-object relation, the production of pieces of work rather than respect for the world as it already exists, the use of instruments, the relationships between one and an imprecisely defined multiple: people, others, nations, etc, the representation of the universe as made up of abstractions, the past tense.

The fact that similar features appear in various languages and cultures, with secondary differences, is very interesting as regards training in multicultural coexistence, since it represents a process that can be universalized.

*

Democracy Begins Between Two

But an education in citizenship requires, in my view, both respect for, and the development of, the specific characteristics of man and woman, as well as an apprenticeship in dialogue between them, with each gender retaining its own tendencies and modifying them in the exchange with the other.

Training in citizenship involves changes in, or at least additions to, educational programmes. It has to be borne in mind that the subject is two, not one, and that it is a question of educating two subjects, without forgetting to develop coexistence, dialogue, and even love between them, since this is the task that falls to each citizen, male and female.

So a second thread connects the texts gathered here: the concern to promote a real 'parity' of opportunity in the education of children, of little boys and girls, and also an education in love between the genders as a path towards democracy.

As far as I am concerned, I always try to combine theory with practice. So, for several years now, I've wanted to work alongside a man on cultural and political problems, assuming that these can be separated. I wanted a working collaboration with a man sufficiently close-to yet different-from me that we can be and remain two in a continual dialectic of becoming, whether in relationship or at work, each bringing to the other a part of his or her life hitherto unknown to the other.

Working with Renzo Imbeni in this way on a code of

Introduction

citizenship at the European level, I learnt first of all to cultivate citizenship between us. And I certainly could not have imagined the same project working with a woman only, which does not mean that our proposals are unfavourable to women. Sometimes the process of composing with the other gender is a better way of revealing the problems associated with one's own gender, and how to deal with them. We need difference and negativity in order to perceive things. The relationship between the genders obliges us to adopt this sort of discipline, and to discover ourselves as different in ways that are not simply positive. In my view, work carried out by two genders maintains the dialectical process and the degree of attention that are indispensable if the duality within the respect for difference is to emerge.

Of course, we have to remain two, and this is not that easy. A training in difference within parity of this sort is what I should like to pass on, to adults and young people alike.

The various accounts gathered here have been chosen with a similar desire in mind.

They relate, moreover, to a work written, last year for the most part, with the aim of defining a new kind of citizenship.

The fact that work of this kind has often developed within the framework of Europe does not mean that it is not concerned with the national, regional, everyday level. The construction of Europe helps us to see the urgent necessity of creating a form of citizenship that respects differences. Besides, we are now European citizens. Europe is not beyond us, outside us, alien to us: we are Europe. If we do not wish to abandon the European Union to the sole charge of businessmen and negotiators, or to the custody of countries who are more interested in the process of its construction, we must promote a new citizenship between the men and women who make it up and, first and foremost, between ourselves.

Training in citizenship is not, then, something secondary, a flower that will grow of its own accord out of a great European market. On the contrary, it is a task of the same importance as the economic one, and which should ensure a balance between protecting the identity of male and female citizens, and opening the borders to commercial exchange and the movement of individuals.

In fact, the European Union is making us face the problem of treating as connected matters too often separated in History: the management of goods and the management of people.

We are now living as body, on the one hand, and spirit on the other, divided between State and Church. The necessities of our times, and especially the European Union, are forcing us to deal politically with the union of body and soul, of bodies and souls.

We cannot avoid this, just as we cannot avoid moving beyond the relationships of domination that exist between the sexes, the genders.

Introduction

For this reason, I have, if I may be permitted to say so, and from a pedagogical as well as a personal desire, left both the writing and the pronunciation of the accounts gathered here in their fleshly – if this is the right expression – context.

It remains clear whom I am addressing. The public that I am trying to teach, with whom I am attempting a dialogue, remains visible. I have also retained the almost entirely spoken quality of the discourse.

Most of the texts reproduce the spontaneity of exchanges with Renzo Imbeni, who was often present at the gathering at which the talk was given; some of the texts were even sent to him in written form since this was shared work. So this is not a polished work, in traditional academic style, but a grouping of texts which still live and speak with immediacy and sensitivity. And, I hope, in a civil manner also: they speak of citizenship by attempting to practise it.

Finally, I'd like to thank Renzo Imbeni for being willing to try out a slightly different kind of politics with me. I hope that this sort of daring, which is in keeping with the times, may open the way to a fairer, more fruitful and happier kind of politics.

I'd also like to thank the women of the Commission for Equal Opportunities who invited me to experiment with a new form of citizenship in the region of Emilia Romagna. In this way they offered me a space in which to try out my ideas and proposals. They entrusted me with a considerable task but, at the same time, gave me a wonderful present. I hope that I am up to this task, and that I am worthy of the faith and hospitality shown to me by the President and the Counsellor for Training and Employment in the region.

I Want Love, Not War

My thanks to the friends of the Federation of the PDS of Bologna who invited me to a debate with Renzo Imbeni, four years ago, on the occasion of his election to the European Parliament. They provided the initial impetus, so to speak, for my book *I Love To You*. Without their initiative I would not have come to know Renzo Imbeni as mayor, as member of parliament and as a man. In dedicating my book to him, I have, of course, dedicated it to one of their companions. In Renzo Imbeni, I have acknowledged in one individual the human qualities and the honesty which I have encountered in other members of the PCI and PDS, particularly in the city of Bologna. In honouring Renzo Imbeni I hope to pay homage to the city and to the people of Bologna.

But why, then, you may be wondering, dedicate a book to a man of your country, to a man of your city,

---

Presentation of *I Love to You*, at the invitation of the Federation of the PDS (Bologna, 4 March 1993).

to a man of your party, to one man alone and not, rather, to a group, to a crowd, to a mass, to a city, to an institution?

My reply is a sincere one: because I am a woman, and because my encounter with this man has become a part of my life.

This is true, but it still does not explain why Luce Irigaray, leading theorist of sexual difference, as you say in Italy, should address her work to Renzo Imbeni, an honest mayor, a member of the PDS and a member of the European Parliament. We have to look at things a little more closely if we are to avoid the risk of falling back on the stereotypes concerning relations between men and women.

What I wanted and had to do – both are true – was to sketch a new approach to democracy and, simultaneously, a new form of recognition between man and woman, both aiming at a better state of civil coexistence between them and a greater happiness in History. It seems to me that we are dealing here with the same approach: being a truly democratic man, a truly democratic woman, and recognizing ourselves, between the two of us, as man and woman. This approach is, I believe, the basis for that 'renewal of the moral and democratic foundations' which Renzo Imbeni, in his resignation speech, demanded of the city of Bologna. I am happy to be able to lay one of the first stones as a contribution to this refounding of a city whose spiritual depth can be recognized both in the hearts of its inhabitants and, also, in the very stones of which it is

I Want Love, Not War

made; a city which remains vividly alive in historical memory and now awaits a future that will be the equal of its past, a future that will not betray it, and which is open to the world.

Yet History does not happen of its own accord. It is up to us to build it. This task has become so complex nowadays that it escapes our competence. We are buried, as it were, beneath all our productions, unable to find our way through the present and towards the future. We are in a labyrinth, searching for the light that marks the way out, wondering who and what we are, what humanity is or what it has become, if we have not already given up asking questions altogether and become simply cogs in a machine which functions without us, reduced to numbers in a History which unfolds beyond our control.

In which case, we are no longer human and, in a democratic era, have lost the capacity to govern ourselves. Now democracy means government by each man, by each woman. It is not just a question of trusting this person or that, of saying yes or no to whomever seems to deserve our faith, but of being capable of a project, of a political government; and of requiring that a given individual, male or female, administer the policies which we have chosen.

Renzo Imbeni has shown you that democracy belongs to everyone, male and female, by entrusting the government of the city to you, by making the right of citizenship an active right for all citizens, male and female, and not a right which is passively received with the option of being challenged or revoked.

Renzo Imbeni is a man, a man who, by his training and life history, favours equality. Yet he is capable, in the name of equality, of respecting differences. He has proved this in the decisions which he has made concerning the diversity of religious and sexual choices as, too, in his remarks on the need to avoid forcing a city to submit to national centralization, or an individual to an institution.

I am a woman, a woman who favours difference, even though I understand that equality can, and sometimes must, come first in order that the differences can be seen for what they really are. To be in favour, for example, of the difference between man and woman cannot be interpreted as a return to a hierarchical situation; instead, we have to move into a new era, in which it is recognized that the irreducible core of a community is to be found between a man and a woman who respect each other in their differences.

In our era, men and women meet in public life, and a just form of politics can no longer be based on the institution of the family as such but needs rather a relation of civil coexistence between the masculine and feminine genders. This civil coexistence enables the family, moreover, to be given a new foundation on the basis of words and rights corresponding to a genuinely civil maturity on the part of women as of men.

*

I Want Love, Not War

A man, a woman: in a relationship of civil maturity, this couple can represent the first stone in a 'renewal of the democratic and moral foundations' which cannot be achieved without this base.

A founding gesture of this sort is within the reach of all of us. It does not require special skills, nor money nor possessions, nor that we should be of a particular age. Each of us, male and female, is capable of it. We need only understand that our humanity is not constructed through things external to us but by following the path of interiority, an interiority which is indispensable to us, man and woman, in order to subvert the impact on culture and on love of the unmediated affect which drives us.

Yet this interiority leads to happiness. To be capable of chastity – in a new sense, of course – no longer means avoiding sin, from fear of God or the devil, nor even from fear of judicial penalties, but so that we can be happier in ourselves and amongst us, so that we can build a new form of democratic civilization which is not solely or primarily concerned with the possession of goods but rather, first and foremost, with respect for individual existence.

If this path calls for the refounding of the relationships between man and woman, it also involves refounding the relationships between civilization and religious life, between civilization, thought and art, between civilization and culture.

In my view, accomplishing this task would be democracy's greatest achievement. Yet again, it is within the reach of all of us, male and female, and it entrusts the government of the city, of the civil community, to each and everyone of us.

A democratic politics does not begin with an adding up of 'yeses', with a crowd electing whoever is going to govern them; it can only be based on a two which is not reducible to one plus one abstract individuals, on a two which comes into existence between a man and a woman who meet and respect each other in their irreducibility.

This couple embodies the ultimate concrete reality of the community; and nowadays we have to rethink all forms of community and universality from a basis in a concrete reality. We have to begin from a true concrete universal, that is, from the relationship between a man and a woman who, in faithfulness to their bodily and spiritual differences, maintain the ideal of their own gender in an alliance with the other gender.

My encounter with Renzo Imbeni has led me to hope that this work is possible. During our debate at San Donato some years ago – a debate which I speak of at the start of *I Love To You*, – I sensed that Renzo Imbeni entertained an ideal which could meet mine, and that he was man enough, and I woman enough, for us to be able to remain *between two*.

Of course, this two is not easy to maintain. History has taught us many things but not the most essential: how to remain between two in love and in civilization.

I Want Love, Not War

In trying to accomplish such a task I have had to reread both Marx and Hegel. I have had to tread once more the long path of History. I have almost rediscovered myself in the nakedness of my own nature, which is not the same as a man's. I preferred the alternative of clothing myself, of clothing us, in a civil code, than that I should find myself, that we should find ourselves, once more driven from the earthly paradise by the weight of a sin which can only be redeemed through suffering. Instead of always speaking only on the level of needs: hunger, dereliction, parental support, I have tried to substitute words which are addressed to one who is equal to me, an equal who is different, of another gender.

It has been like learning to speak all over again and I am still only making my first attempts. I understand that we are saying different things although we think we are saying the same things.

I was saying: I want to be together with you, even at work; he, on the contrary: I have to accomplish my task. But, fundamentally, we were both saying: I'd like to achieve my ideal together with you, if this is possible. Between us, the intention and the ideal were able to recover sensitive awareness rather than abandoning it. I understand that woman is usually searching for man where he does not exist; then I remembered the lovers of *The Song of Songs* and wondered what had to be done for man and woman to encounter each other as companions in love, in civil coexistence. I have tried to find my way through tradition but also through some of the gestures, some of the words of this man, Renzo Imbeni, through certain signs of his identity, certain signs that were intended for me and of which I wanted to be worthy.

I have searched hard for a way of recognizing the other: man, whose body and spirit remain unknown to me. I have had to renounce all forms of possessiveness, of appropriation, never saying *me* or *mine* when speaking of the other. I have begun to say 'I love to you' rather than 'I love you'.

I have tried to discover new words that preserve sensitive awareness in the working out of a civil and political relationship.

I have called on the assistance of nature, of culture, of silence, of song, of philosophy and of poetry.

Today I offer you the first steps, the first stage, of this labour of love in the service of a new politics, both private and public, of a new History bringing greater happiness.

I have decided to share my experience for the sake of a political ideal, of a human ideal. I have taken the risk, of course, of offering a singular experience to the public. I want it to remain singular. And I am inviting you to do the same: to search for whatever it is that, for you, represents the place of a singularity which harbours the seed of the universal.

The universal cannot be reached outside the self; it is not a sum of individuals, a multiplicity of cultures, an

I Want Love, Not War

accumulation of possessions. The universal is not so immense that it escapes you. The universal is within you and develops out of you as a flower grows from the earth.

I will add one last thing: the universal is two: it is woman, it is man. And it is found in the encounter between these two universals. At this crossroads, or in this cradle, which is both natural and cultural, humanity can be born or reborn.

This birth or rebirth is possible in faithfulness to ourselves, woman and man, and in listening to the other, with whom we share the task of bringing humanity into being, not only as natural offspring, but also as spiritual children, as humanity and History, present and future.

Finally, I should like to thank Renzo Imbeni for sustaining, in his way, the freedom of my thought, of my writing and of my dedication to him of *I Love To You*. True, this is what I would expect of a mayor of Bologna who does his job properly: the seal of the city bears the term *Libertas* twice over.

Feminine Identity: Biology or Social Conditioning?

The topic which I have been asked to deal with lies at the root of significant conflicts within the women's liberation movement. I shall attempt to deal with it by sketching in the origins of what seems to me a false dilemma.

Many initiatives emerged from the cultural revolution of 1968, from a human liberation movement which involved the liberation of women as women.

Amongst them was the movement 'Choice'.[1] At that time, neither 'Choice' nor those of us who were fighting on the barricades, in the strict or perhaps slightly more symbolic sense of the term, posed the question of whether we were there in the name of our female body or as a result of social conditioning. We were fighting a battle for civil and cultural rights appropriate to our difference and, above all, for the right to abortion, which is linked with our biological identity.

Paper presented at the Colloquium 'For a Democracy of Parity', at the invitation of the movement 'Choice' (Paris, 3 June 1993).

Feminine Identity: Biology or Social Conditioning?

We were fighting to be recognized as women and to achieve a form of human freedom corresponding to our feminine identity. We conducted our struggle in order to have freedom of choice concerning pregnancy, and also to try and ensure that our bodies were protected against all the forms of violence threatening them, rape being the most obvious.

In order to win rights of this sort, which are closely tied up with that of being in charge, in a civilized way, of our female body, we joined forces democratically. We were women enough and strong enough to obtain crucial legislative changes in favour of women's liberation, although we were not in a majority in the competent assemblies. Some women, Simone Veil in particular, and some men, too, gave us their active support and helped get the first draft of a civil code in feminine mode through Parliament.

This was a great deal at the time. But it was still not enough to accomplish the kind of peaceful civil revolution that the women's liberation movement brought with it. In fact, any rights gained were still expressed in terms of permission granted within the context of a patriarchal family: family understood in the narrow sense, political or religious family. So, for example, we were granted permission to have abortions without being punished or penalized, but not yet given the positive right to freedom of choice concerning pregnancy. Similarly, any rights gained had to bear a masculine stamp of approval to have any real value. Rape was categorized as a crime, is still termed a crime, which effectively eliminates the problem of respect for the female body as such and in no way alerts the potential rapist to the felony that his action represents.

Many other rights which are essential if women are to be granted a civil identity, a sovereignty of citizenship that satisfies the requirements of a democratic society, were lacking: the right to a culture in feminine mode with its own linguistic and religious values; the right to public and political representation and delegations; specific rights to help mothers with the custody and education of their children, particularly in the case of intercultural or separated couples; and adequate rights concerning work.

A civil code in feminine mode is what the militants of 1968 were asking for. Their determination to be recognized as women was the power behind their public protest wherever it occurred.

Women's struggles which, in an initial phase, found themselves outside, or even opposed to, the machinery of State and party, untouched by questions of money and power, have gradually spread through contact with women established in public organizations and political bodies. The revolutionary message of 1968 which was simple and clear, and which any woman in France, Europe or throughout the world, could understand, has been complicated by institutional strategies and politico-cultural debates dependent on a language or a logic which no longer speaks to the mass of women. It has become caught up in conflicts that have nothing to do

Feminine Identity: Biology or Social Conditioning?

with the impertinent claims of the militants of 1968. 'We want love, not war', for example, was one of the subversive slogans of the time. 'Imagination in power' another. And, voicing women's concerns only: 'The private is political' or 'Our bodies are no longer your capital'.

The request for the right to a specific civil identity for women has been even more toned down in the years since the 1980s. 'France has opted for equality rather than difference', I heard a journalist for a French weekly newspaper calmly claiming on the occasion of a conference organized by the School of Parents and Teachers in the Ile-de-France (Ecole des parents et des éducateurs en Ile-de-France). The choice of a masculinist strategy of this sort explains a great deal about the ebbing of the tide which carried the women's movement born in 1968: the retreat from the gains made by women in the name of their difference, the collapse of the solidarity established between the women who fought together up until October 1978 for the right to free and self-determined contraception and abortion, the loss of what had been the goal of the national and international women's campaigns which grew out of the cultural revolution, in other words, the right to a civil identity as women.

The issues have become so attenuated that the idea of becoming a woman is looked on now as out of date, reactionary, shameful. To be or become a woman tends to be viewed as the effect of a social conditioning to be analyzed and overcome, rather than as a desire to be cultivated and offered for recognition: that of belonging to a different sex or gender that makes up half the human species.

Women who had only just left patriarchal families, whether private or public, were starting to awaken to a different identity, an identity of their own. It was not very difficult to send some of them back into the home and to reduce the others to silence by depriving them of a place in which to speak or by offering them access to money and power in masculine mode on condition that they alter their way of thinking and behaving.

Patriarchal power has, moreover, rallied support for an ideal of equality by appealing to another bloodier revolution which had nothing to do with women's right to be different.

So women's activities and accomplishments on behalf of women have become bland, formulated in a neutral manner, expressing themselves as a claim to have the same rights as men. Many women have, in this way, taken on an economic, cultural and political conditioning that belongs to a masculine identity and History. They have sacrificed their own identity as women or that of their sisters in order to conform, or make their sisters conform, to a socio-historical conditioning that is man's.

Women's struggles have thus lost their popular, democratic character: by adopting the opinions and power of those, male or female, who had the right to speak, they have abandoned the mainstream in favour of academia, colloquia, literary conventions or political groupings. Their own sex, their own gender have become, yet again, a burden for women, and the term 'feminism' is once more the target of mockery or repression. And it is not only men, the media or advertising who are responsible for this, but women themselves, younger women who are almost allergic to the term because they want to live as they wish, to love according to their own desires, to try and construct a history, particularly a sexual history, in feminine mode, judging the problems of women's liberation a thing of the past.

There are many who want to impress such an opinion upon them. Yet these young women, who are able to profit from women's struggles at the economic and juridical level, reject the cultural gains of feminism without any sense of gratitude. They do not want to have to make the effort to renounce the female condition, they do not feel guilty, at least not in a conscious way, for being women; but they are often very isolated, each woman left to herself, facing the difficulties of their love life, for example, rather like orphans, and refusing to say anything to you about them unless you promise not to preach in the name of feminism.

Of course, they prefer either to remain invisible or to blow their own trumpets. They do not really trust mature women: it is only with reluctance that they place their faith in them or vote for them, and it does not take much for them to succumb once more to the stereotypes of phallocratic and even patriarchal power.

Democracy Begins Between Two

It is true that we have left them a rather meagre inheritance, especially in France: there are very few centres where women can meet and talk, for example, and hardly any subsidies or municipal facilities for their cultural activities. In other countries, parity has at least offered this form of hospitality and help for women.

Moreover, we have left younger women very few words on the subject of a different way of being and of loving, on how to go on being yourself, without constant conflict, when in a relationship with the other gender. We still have to achieve this patient construction of an identity in feminine mode, with all that it requires in the way of juridical and cultural mediation, on our own behalf, as more or less young Western women, as well as for women of other cultures where the affirmation of women's autonomy and women's speech is even more difficult than for us. What we ourselves still lack, as do all women, is that greater civil maturity which would entrust us with rights and responsibilities in the context of the couple and the family, but also in all public places.

The question as to whether belonging to a gender is the effect of a biological destiny or of social conditioning fails to take into account the fact that being or becoming a woman means acquiring a civil dimension which is appropriate to 'feminine identity', a culture which corresponds to one's own body and specific genealogy, one's own way of loving and of procreating, of desiring

Feminine Identity: Biology or Social Conditioning?

and of thinking. Feminism's blindest alley is to force women into a deconditioning which strips them of their feminine identity in order to attain an undifferentiated state of universality to be shared in a masculine or neutral world.

Yet the prospect of a neutral, asexual community is disturbing. Besides the difficulty of loving each other in neutral mode, and the conflicts arising from who has more or less, man or woman, which develop here according to various sadomasochistic modalities, a society in neutral mode loses sight of the line separating life from death. Although life, obviously, is always sexed, death on the contrary no longer makes this distinction.

A society which eliminates the dividing line between life and death is capable of all forms of holocaust. It no longer takes a particular individual, whether evil or mad, or one form of political regime rather than another, to produce them; they occur quite simply because we have lost sight of the boundary separating life from death.

This is the point that we have reached today. The reign in neutral mode of a technological, technocratic era will be of no use to us in a moment of such peril. The sharing out of political responsibility can only help to bring about some change here if it is founded on two different identities, proof that we are living men and living women and not individuals in the abstract, impersonal, rather like robots or strange beings beyond the reach of death.

The step which women have to take is to obtain positive rights of citizenship in female mode.

Democracy assumes the sovereignty of every citizen. Yet neither dictionaries nor civil codes take into consideration the fact that female citizens account for more than half the total number of citizens. The right which has to be established or re-established as first condition of a democratic regime, is the right to exist or to be oneself with sovereignty. Such a right is, as yet, non-existent for women who, at best, are permitted to present themselves as neutral or assimilable to men, as reproductive nature or as productive manpower, in a community where, as women, they go unrecognized.

The necessary and right thing to do, before trying to establish oneself in institutions whose democratic character needs to be rethought, is to demand the right to civil maturity, the right to represent oneself before that of representing other women, while still lacking the juridical criteria which sanction one's own identity.

A right to civil maturity of this sort should be universal as long as it is borne in mind that the universal is two, masculine and feminine. A right of this sort is indispensable to ensure that each woman can and must exist as such.

Such a right to civil maturity requires a refashioning of the juridical codes: Civil Code, Constitution, Penal Code and the Universal Declaration of Human Rights. It also calls for a reassessment of the boundaries separating natural and civil law.

*

Feminine Identity: Biology or Social Conditioning?

To bring a community made up of sovereign male and female citizens into being would be a fine democratic task for women to accomplish, and one which would, in addition, respect the first steps which they have taken towards their own liberation.

Of course, it is no longer a question of obtaining, nor even of promising, power in no matter what shape or form. Democracy cannot have its basis in any form of power, even if shared, other than one in which men and women coexist as sovereign beings: a woman *or* a man, capable of sharing a right of this sort to exist in a community made up of women *and* men. Democracy begins through a civil relationship, protected by rights, between a man and a woman, a male citizen and a female citizen, each and every citizen.

Women's Enslavement

Five good-hearted, great-hearted people are seated at this table.[2] Forgive me if I count myself amongst them. But since a bond of affection already links me to the other four, I can no longer exclude myself without causing them pain. So here we are, five great-hearted people, and there is much that we can do together, and with all of you, men and women, together.

We can do it wholeheartedly, with kindness and courtesy, not through conflict and violence which are out of keeping, in my view, with the basic Italian character.

The setting of man against woman or woman against man is particularly out of keeping with this character.

Some countries, for example, have either a male or a female patron-saint and people sometimes joke about this alternation.

Italy, kindly, has chosen the guardianship of a couple: Francis of Assisi and Catherine of Siena, a couple who

---

Talk given at the national Festival of Unity, at the invitation of Livia Turco and of the Federation of the PDS (Bologna, 17 September 1993).

should have been enemies given the conflict between Franciscans and Dominicans. But together they watch over Italy and safeguard your country even despite Papal wishes when necessary.

They are not, then, Catholics, subject to Church power, but subversive cultural and political figures in your historical tradition. They created Italian history and one should not forget how they did it, nor the meaning of what they have passed down to us.

I do not know how long this guardianship of Italy by a couple has existed, but it strikes me as beautiful and intelligent.

As well as Francis of Assisi and Catherine of Siena, there are also Laura and Petrarch, Dante and Beatrice. And undoubtedly other couples that I have forgotten.

Italy seems to want to be assisted by couples rather than by a man or a woman, men or women.

So you can see from this why *I Love To You*, from historical necessity, is dedicated to an Italian, to Italy.

Yet it is not enough simply to remember; it is our duty to continue History and not only by repeating it. We have to build the present and the future while remaining faithful to the past and, once again from historical necessity, this past and this future must nowadays be shaped anew by men and women, working in a new way amongst themselves. This is a difficult task but a necessary and a worthwhile one.

If we want to create a democratic politics, if we want

to overcome the alienation present in religious traditions, we have to rethink the relationships between man and woman, men and women.

I would say that historically this is our task, that of all women and men. We cannot run away from it without running away from ourselves.

In *I Love To You*, more than in my other books, I have initiated this path towards a new love between men and women. I have tried to open up a new way for us to love each other. A way that would safeguard our sensibility, feelings, bodies, but that would lead to the acquisition of a new citizenship for woman and for man, and between man and woman, a citizenship made up of respect, of recognition of difference, of differences, and of the discovery of the spiritual fecundity – cultural and political, for example, and not purely natural – of such differences.

In talking of the passage from natural life to civil and spiritual life, I have touched on the key theme of my discourse today: how to cultivate the natural as two, man and woman, and how to pass from natural to civil life together, man and woman, men and women.

For example, we forget every day, because it is simply part of our habits and customs, that woman is still subjected to the state of nature.

She does not yet have the civil right to manage her own nature for herself. She is still subject to the decisions of the State, and in a different way, of the

Women's Enslavement

Church, concerning maternity, for example, and ways of loving and of representing herself.

Political and religious wars are waged over the natural qualities of women, their capacity to love and to procreate in their own body. History has, to a great extent, been built on these natural properties of women. Yet if History is not willing to entrust woman, women, with responsibility towards their own nature, it is pursuing its path with one foot in nature and the other in culture, unfolding in the mode of a master's domination over slaves, male and female.

In Paris at the moment, three weekly newspapers refer to slavery. I wonder whether they have considered the fact that slavery exists amongst us, and is not just something that affects other countries, other peoples, other races, as you might imagine from the cover stories. Slavery is ours, not in a merely symbolic sense but absolutely. Woman is, from birth, a slave until she is able to decide for herself as a civil person. This is how it still is for us today.

At the outset of their liberation movement, women knew that they were slaves and established as the objective of their struggles: how to escape from slavery.

They asked for rights, civil rights of existence as women, in order to carry out this task. Indeed anyone, man or woman, who does not enjoy specific rights, who is subject to the rights of others, is a slave. I myself, for example, am still a slave with respect to the civil codes currently in force.

Affection, and fine words, and even being allowed a job, important or unimportant, in the world of men are not enough to console me: I remain a slave. I am not talking metaphorically here but of a civil reality of which we are not sufficiently aware.

No law grants me the right to exist as a woman. And no neutral law grants me it either. Certain decisions which determine my life are subject to the civil power of others: the decision to have a child, for example.

I am not talking about an agreement between those who love each other, the woman, and the man who is the father of the child. It is the State, and in a different way the Church, who can decide, in other words who can take the civil decision on the woman's behalf. She is left with the natural state of the body, at best with the emotional potential of her subjectivity, but as a woman she remains a slave of the civil power insofar as the decision to have a child is concerned. This enslavement weighs indirectly on the couple, on couples.

In my view, 'permission to have an abortion', instead of the right to choose for herself whether to be a mother or not, is already a formulation which fails to allow the woman civil responsibility for maternity, and already considers her only within the confines of her natural state.

I have given this example because it is politically very important, fundamental even, for the becoming of History, and yet it remains completely unresolved in many of our countries. Yet it is not all right to move forward

Women's Enslavement

unless we have obtained the right for women themselves to choose to be mothers.

One could argue along the same lines for all forms of sexual violence.

You know, as I do, all the distractions that political powers, capitalist regimes, in the narrow or wider economic sense, are capable of inventing to divert attention from the way they control the body and nature of woman.

And women allow themselves to be fascinated and ensnared once again by proposals and presents that rank second to their emergence from slavery. For example: a powerful position in contemporary society dazzles them; or: they allow themselves to be seduced by the possibility of running civil society along with men before enjoying the right to exist themselves in a civil fashion.

Even the right to work should be, for women, a path towards their release from slavery and not simply a means of access to an economic identity. The latter ought to be the means of changing awareness with regard to civil autonomy, and not simply a right to work as a slave in the world of work as it exists today.

I believe that you, women and men gathered here, should be able to understand the problem and to take a stand against the enslavement of women, and of all those who love each other and who suffer, through women, because of this enslavement. I believe that you are capable of understanding that this enslavement is part of a power game which resembles and, in fact, is identical to, the one against which you are fighting your battles.

Marxists have often faced the objection that they are only concerned with goods and not with people. I believe that today, at the point in History which we have reached, you, we, are able to rise to a challenge: the desire for justice which burnt so strongly in the hearts of Marxists must not be allowed to die but, quite the reverse, must extend to all the ways by which individuals are made slaves, of which economic slavery is only one.

I have spoken of the necessity for women to move from the state of nature to civil life, if they are to escape from slavery. This is equally true, as I have said, for couples, for all who love each other in the flesh.

But today there are also other places where a similar gesture has to be made: to move from belonging to a race to belonging to a wider civil community, for example. This transition is necessary to escape sexism as, too, racism and all forms of power which, in fact, share the same roots: a flaw in the relation between the state of nature and civil identity which makes civil coexistence impossible. The question of women is not, then, in this respect, any different from the question of racism; in fact, one could say – as the militant feminists of the 1970s did – that it is the most fundamental one, and that dealing with it in our own countries will help us to know what to do in other contexts.

To pass from the state of nature to civil life without abandoning the relationship with nature – that nature which surrounds us, which constitutes us as bodies, sexed bodies, as woman and man, – a gesture of this kind was the project of my last book, *I Love To You*. It tells of my encounter with Renzo Imbeni and, after arguing that a double nature exists, a masculine and a feminine nature, I try to find a way of making an alliance between these two natures possible without one being subordinated to the other. I explain the necessity of a sexed right to clothe us in civil life and, simply, to enable us to respect each other in love. I also try to find new words and new gestures for us to be able to speak to and listen to each other in the recognition of our difference, a recognition which initially leaves us without words, simply listening to the mystery of the other, male or female. I also ask how we can rethink our tradition, particularly the religious one, in order to be able to love each other here below, making of the other a horizontal transcendence, an absolute which cannot be gone beyond insofar as it is irreducible to oneself.

I have continued the work of *I Love To You* for two years. It is demanding but also makes me happy. Like *Speculum*, it is a historical task that cannot remain mine alone but has to be the work of many, women and men.

*

Democracy Begins Between Two

I hope that we will be adequate to this task, particularly we women and men who wish to be democratic and faithful to certain figures of the Italian Left who deserve our respect.

How to Manage the Transition from Natural to Civil Coexistence?

Every time that we step beyond the horizon of the known, the horizon of our habits, each time that we move into a new and wider sphere, one that reaches beyond our past and our present, it would be useful to reassure ourselves that we can turn back, that we are still on dry land, that we are not crossing the point of no return.

In constructing the European Union, for example, we have to see to it that each of us, male and female, remains capable of a return to the self, a return to the self not in the sense of identity as national, ethnic, cultural, etc. but in terms of human identity.

A few years ago, saying that the end of the world or, at least, a turning-point for our civilization, had come was seen as symptomatic of some personal pathology.

Talk given at the conference 'European Citizenship', organized by Renzo Imbeni, at the invitation of the PDS delegation of the Group for the Unitary European Left (Bologna, 22–23 October 1993).

Democracy Begins Between Two

Times have changed to such an extent that most people now hold the opposite point of view; many believe and reiterate that we have reached a critical moment as far as shared existence in a community, the future of the planet, the survival of life and, in particular, of the human species are concerned.

Of course, there are still some who, to reassure themselves and sometimes us, claim that this is just one more historical or cosmic cycle amongst so many others. But such claims are becoming less arrogant, more timid.

The question has, then, to be asked: what is to be done? And: how is it to be done?

There is no doubt that anxiety, and not only economic anxiety, causes either a retreat into individualism or a worrying degree of gregariousness.

What remedy can be found for this double movement which threatens the organization of a civil community, especially when it is enlarged and becomes more complex: a community on the scale, for example, of Europe?

The European Union forces us to face economic problems which are not, apparently, beyond our mental grasp: though they may be complicated, they are familiar to us, or at least to some of us. However, the European Union presents us with difficulties which, though more within our reach, appear insurmountable because they have come to seem alien to us, even though they are part of our daily life, of our emotions, of the surroundings in which we live. In fact, what is closest or nearest to us strikes us today as the thing that is

Managing Transition from Natural to Civil Coexistence?

hardest to conceive of, either because we have got used to thinking rather about the distant and the abstract, leaving what is near to the inertia of habit, or because to think about what surrounds us requires us, more often than not, to reinterpret our habits, our way of being; in other words, ourselves.

Undoubtedly the constant mobility which modern life, and especially the European Union, encourages, though offering certain advantages, also comes up against the danger of driving further away our ability to return to ourselves, of distancing us a little more from our human identity.

This perhaps explains why so many citizens, male and female, are afraid of the opening-up of frontiers made necessary by the construction of Europe. There are vital reasons for this fear and many people feel, in a blind sort of way, that today the survival of the human species is threatened. I think that it is a mistake to deny such a misgiving rather than attempting to define ways of dispelling it.

In my view, this misgiving is provoked by the unconscious fear that entry into an enlarged community will increase the split between our belonging to a natural state and the new citizenship, or by the fear that this citizenship will dissolve natural identity into an abstract identity managed by others – not us, not me, – beyond the reach of our or my decisions, of our or my freedom.

So it is necessary, I believe, to make a way of returning to the self available in proportion to the distancing from self which entry into an enlarged community implies.

I shall try, then, to propose a definition of European citizenship which takes this requirement into account.

The natural survival of the human species has, for centuries, been entrusted, above all, to the family: it produces or reproduces life, shelters it, maintains it. This social unit represents the place of production and custody of living beings without whom neither Italy nor Europe can exist, let alone discover their own meaning.

This social unit also represents the place of the return to the state of nature, not only through reproduction and the raising of children but also through bodily and carnal relationships, emotional life, physical rest and regeneration.

Yet, in the family, individual identity is lost; the family is a unity, it constitutes an undifferentiated one in which each male, each female alienates his/her own identity. The cause of this, in my view, is the lack of a passage, within the family itself, from natural to civil identity.

Other places function in the same way as the family: the State and the Church, for example.

Now the family unit has been called into question in our era and so, also, the structures connected with it, the Church and the State. This means that the traditional organization of the relationships between

Managing Transition from Natural to Civil Coexistence?

nature and culture, between nature and citizenship, is in crisis. We are already witnessing, within cities and nations, a falling back on groups based on the state of nature: on belonging to a particular age-group, sex or race. This regression to a tribal form of organization – as certain sociologists refer to it – represents an obstacle to civil coexistence because it divides the community into groups which do not communicate amongst themselves, and between whom, on the contrary, aggression increases. This can already be seen on the horizontal level of coexistence between citizens and, in a certain sense, it runs the risk of duplicating itself on the model of net-like structures, if these latter develop only on the level of social sedimentation and so fail to ensure the homogeneity of the civil community. The task of connecting natural and civil coexistence is therefore particularly urgent if we are to move towards an enlarged community such as the European Union.

At least three examples of potential crises hover around the question of European citizenship:
– coexistence between races, even within the family itself;
– coexistence between the sexes, even of differing traditions;
– coexistence between generations of different ages.

In all three cases, the emergence of a natural category of belonging – race, sex, age – calls coexistence between citizens into question.

Denying that the problem exists, or covering it over

with a variety of economic or cultural constructions, resolves nothing and runs the risk of allowing the nucleuses to become contaminated by potential conflicts.

Nor does neutralizing the difference serve any purpose, other than a loss of human identity.

So we are forced to confront the emergence of a state of nature in which civil identity and coexistence are, as yet, lacking, a state of nature which is linked to race, sex, generation or age. Faced with such a development, either we return to a natural form of coexistence whether familial, tribal or ethnic and, in another mode, religious, cultural or state-related, or we mould this state of nature according to abstract norms which deny it and fail to dissolve its potential for violence.

In fact, forcing races, sexes and generations to conform to a single model of identity, culture and civilization means subjecting them to an order which does not respect their differences. One could then speak of a new way of colonizing, of evangelizing, of imposing the guardianship of a wealthy patriarch, not only on the level of money but also of civilization. The enlarged community would then develop on the basis of the compassion felt by the richer members, in the cultural sense also, for the poorer, in the direction of a sharing of their goods.

But I am not sure that the poorest will accept such aid, nor that aid of this sort actually contributes towards safeguarding them and their growth.

In any case, paternalism of this kind does not ensure

Managing Transition from Natural to Civil Coexistence?

a horizontal coexistence between us all, male and female.

In order to define a European citizenship, it is therefore essential to consider and to articulate at least three places of transition and of coexistence between natural and civil life.

The economic sphere cannot solve the problem. It has always tried to deny it. But today this is no longer possible and the economic dynamic has made what it wanted to conceal emerge into the light of day. The presence in the labour market of emigrants, women, young people, has made very obvious how these people are, in fact, treated in the framework of the state of nature: in the family or in other modes of natural coexistence. I am not referring only to the difficulties linked with the job market itself, with the remuneration of labour, but also to civil coexistence, to relationships of citizenship. There are factories in France, for example, where women went on strike with the sole aim of achieving recognition of their civil status, and not for an increase in wages.

How has this emergence of the state of nature been possible in our cultured traditions?

The opposition between natural law and civil rights, which regulates our legislation, would seem to account for quite a bit.

Natural law has, for the most part, been left to the

custody of the family. The latter, as I have already remarked, is supposed to produce and protect life. It is also meant to ensure coexistence between the individuals who make it up: natural or private coexistence, as it is referred to, in which the State has no powers of direct intervention. This natural coexistence is based, first and foremost, on the body of the woman, on her procreative properties, on her qualities as mother and, in a secondary manner, as wife. This natural coexistence also involves children's bodies, and the feelings between mother and child. Only one part of man belongs to natural coexistence: the part of sexual desire, and of the marital and paternal authority linked to it. Another part of man moves between natural and civil coexistence and, as such, enjoys civil rights which are not, however, appropriate to women and children.

The passage from natural to civil coexistence takes place through the family itself by means of property, goods, money, and not by means of the rights of individuals. The State, it is argued, must not intervene in the private sphere. Obviously it intervenes in the production of children as, too, in the payment of taxes and in the financial assistance associated with procreation. But, in the relations between individuals, it should not intervene . . .

Our civil codes do not wish to have anything to do with natural coexistence. This explains why they are virtually silent concerning the rights of individuals as such. When it is a question of such rights, they become

Managing Transition from Natural to Civil Coexistence?

as abstract and as imprecise as is necessary to avoid any definition of singular civil status.

In this way they become incomprehensible to citizens when speaking of the rights of individuals or between individuals. In contrast, when it comes to the ownership of goods, they are concrete, prolix, rich in singular detail.

The qualities of goods seem to mask those of individuals, and ownership seems to take the place of the desire to exist, and of care for life itself.

Some goods help, undeniably, to protect life: the house, for example. But the goods necessary to life have multiplied to such an extent that they have ended up taking the place of life itself. We know all too well that money and presents can be substituted for carnal desire which is often sacrificed, moreover, to work, on the one hand, and to procreation on the other.

A culture of life does not, in fact, exist. A culture of the body, a culture of the natural sensibility, a culture of ourselves as living beings, is still lacking.

This question arises, moreover, in a period of History which sets itself the goal of redefining the relationship with the other: the primitive, the child, the mad person, the disabled person, the worker and, finally, the woman.

We have tried to group all of these together within the category of the other, that other towards whom the white man, now of age, the competent white man, should behave with compassion.

Democracy Begins Between Two

But this feeling of almost religious pity is, more often than not, unable to stand up to the sexual instincts, the instinct of possession, and is too often forgotten when the economic market is at stake.

Besides, the other, male or female, has no desire to be beholden to us. Nothing is worse, according to Hegel, than compassion in politics. It implies that the gap between rich and poor is growing. I am fairly much in agreement with him on this point, and I believe that the compassion currently demonstrated by our politicians can often be interpreted as a desire for hierarchical domination which adopts the guise of patriarchal benevolence. Even if the well-intentioned amongst our politicians are unaware of it, this gesture risks maintaining a vertical hierarchy in the civil community.

For me, the way to overcome such a hierarchy is through recourse to the right to civil identity: a positive, affirmative right enjoyed by every person irrespective of sex, race or age.

To enjoy the right to exist, to be oneself, male or female, in a sovereign manner, outside a master-slave relationship, could be protected by a civil code which placed the emphasis on the individual's right to identity

A code of this sort would enable us to overcome the differences between the sexes, the races, the generations, so that we could have access to a civil identity not subject to natural norms.

A right of this sort does not, however, mean the

Managing Transition from Natural to Civil Coexistence?

imposition of an abstract, neutral identity. Natural differences continue to exist when they form part of a specific identity and when they are necessary to our existence as civil individuals. This is particularly evident as regards sexual difference. But the difference, the differences between women and men are redefined through a civil code which recognizes the singularity of the individual yet entrusts him/her with duties towards the self and towards others.

A civil right like this entrusts women, for example, but also other races and young people, with the obligation to behave as adults capable of rationality and of coexistence.

So the woman does not remain the daughter – nor the mother – of the husband, and the Black does not remain the son of the white man. To be recognized as a civil person, female or male, compels each to safeguard his/her singularity, but also to educate it to subdue the sensibility and unmediated instinct.

A passage of this sort from the state of nature to civil life seems to me the only way towards defining citizenship for Europe. If we succeed in doing this, we will be taking yet another step in the process of humanity's, and each individual's, becoming. Europe would then offer an opportunity not only for economic development, but for the growth of each and everyone of us, within the family itself, within the city and in every relationship between us.

Towards a Citizenship of the European Union

Five years ago, the Federation of the then PCI of Bologna summoned me to a meeting with Renzo Imbeni, the mayor of the city and a candidate for the European elections. We had a very lively encounter, with a genuine debate between the two of us, and neither side seeking the subjection or the submission of the other.

During this meeting, which I describe at the start of *I Love To You*, a book dedicated to him, I had requested Renzo Imbeni to undertake to obtain new rights in favour of individuals, in particular of women: the right to physical and moral integrity, the right to the free choice of maternity, the right to human dignity, the right for a mother in certain cases to have privileged custody of her children, the right to work and to a culture that are appropriate, etc.

When Renzo Imbeni, as a member of the European Parliament, was given responsibility last year, in the

---

Work carried out as a duo by Renzo Imbeni and Luce Irigaray (May 1993–January 1994).

framework of the Commission for Civil Liberties and Internal Affairs, for reporting on citizenship of the Union, he let me know that he was willing for us to work together.

While he began defining the content of his *Report*, I conceived of the *Draft Code of Citizenship*. Originally envisaged as a shared work, this *Draft* drew its inspiration from the two people involved, from their experience of life and work and, in particular, from their political choices. So, although it was written by me, it was possible to sign the text with both our names.

I should add that, at the same time, I had requested that both Renzo Imbeni and myself be appointed to the Planning Group of the European Parliamentary Commission. With this aim in mind, I was invited to submit a two-page proposal. Hence, the proportions of the *Draft Code of Citizenship*.

Although the emphasis placed on the civil dimension attracted the attention of the experts, advisers to Jacques Delors, they made no concrete proposals to collaborate at that point. Some, at least, even showed reservations concerning the necessity of rights to protect civil relationships. Such resistance can perhaps be explained by the fact that, before the Treaty of Maastricht, the European Parliament did not have the right to legislate supranationally and that the strategy was to avoid all jurisprudential problems which might interfere with the competence of the national codes.

*

Democracy Begins Between Two

But the Treaty of Maastricht, which came into effect on November 1st 1993, includes pointers in the direction of rights for European citizens. Above all it includes an article (art. 8.1) which states: 'Citizenship of the Union is instituted'. But this citizenship remains to be defined to a large extent. Since Renzo Imbeni had reported on European citizenship last year, it was his responsibility to try and give it a valid content.

We took this work on together, very interesting work but which also comes up against numerous difficulties, because it deals with a topic all too often neglected: the civil relationships between individuals. It also uncovers the most hidden roots of nationalism: the refusal to question and change one's own habits in the interests of living alongside each other and avoiding conflict and war.

The proposals for a code of citizenship at the European level simultaneously arouse enormous, almost passionate, interest yet also fear, distrust and scepticism as to whether in our world any decisions can still be made by individual men and women. Now this coincides with our wishes: to entrust each man and each woman with a political assignment which extends from their most personal life to the construction of a supranational community.

Towards a Citizenship of the European Union

THE DRAFT CODE OF CITIZENSHIP

The code of citizenship was drawn up from two intersecting intentions:

– To recommend a series of fundamental requirements for forming a citizenship which could be realized in our time, particularly at the level of Europe: a citizenship which would be multicultural, multiracial, multinational, etc.

– To imagine a project which could be shared as a common political task by a man and a woman belonging to two distinct genders, two histories, two cultural upbringings, two political horizons, two languages, two nations, etc...

Indeed, the two intentions coincide: Renzo Imbeni and Luce Irigaray are European citizens in the making. A draft code of citizenship which could be signed by both implied, for each of us and between us, all the elements mentioned whether at the level of the personal or at the level of work.

This draft is not, therefore, intended as a formal, abstract, to some extent arbitrary project, defined by us to be proposed or imposed on a European scale. In its conception, it is a code of citizenship which I addressed to Renzo Imbeni to find out if it was possible to work together politically while remaining man and woman, Italian and French, a man who dedicates his life to a political responsibility within the sphere of institutions and of a party, and a woman who devotes herself to a cultural commitment by practising a politics of liberation, particularly of women, up till now outwith all parties and institutions.

In other words, this code is intended to be practised by each of us, and between us. Working together was an answer to the challenge that we were capable of being civil-minded without relinquishing our sensibility as man and woman, our political and cultural sensibility.

The adventure is sometimes difficult, but thrilling and fruitful. Perhaps it is the only way of establishing a civil code, whether one is dealing with customary law or written rights: to try to define or redefine all the points which are necessary for practising coexistence between us in a civil manner, ma(e)n and woma(e)n of various nations and cultures. It is worth adding, here, that neither Renzo Imbeni nor Luce Irigaray enjoys having recourse to penalties: the remedy for all minor errors is sought in even more civilized behaviour and not in sanctions.

But every man and every woman is, in fact, a bearer of universality, especially if the relationship between them touches on the civil dimension. In writing a civil code for us and for the between-us, I have defined elements of a code which is valid at the European level, and perhaps beyond it.

This code deals above all with civil behaviour as the condition of a public, and also in a certain sense private, relationship, that is of a civil relationship between a man and a woman, but also as a place for safeguarding and protecting human identity as such, and coexistence in the community.

We, men and women, are more and more torn between various identities: natural, economic, social, political, cultural, etc. and it seems therefore vitally urgent to discover a way of safeguarding an identity for us, a place where each of us can remain one. Civil identity can guarantee this place of unity for us, between us and at the community level. Civil identity offers the advantage, moreover, of emphasizing the relationship to the person rather than the relationship to goods, in other words to property or to possession in relationships with ourselves or between us. In this way, emphasizing civil identity comes up against another necessity of our era: that of defining an identity that can also be shared by the unemployed, those who own no property, the marginalized, adolescents, old people.

With this objective, which is the most democratic possible, civil identity would be defined at the intersection of individual, natural identity and of community, relational identity, a transition which each person, male and female, would have to make on their own behalf and consent to the other, male or female.

Now, on at least three levels, the establishment of the European Union will depend on the intersection between the state of nature and civil coexistence: on the

Democracy Begins Between Two

level of relations between men and women, on the level of relations between generations and on the level of relations between the races. Not long ago, and still today in certain cultures, natural identity was safeguarded and framed by many forms of family: the family in the narrow sense but also the clan, the tribe and even national, cultural, religious families, etc.

For various reasons, these family entities are today in crisis, or their boundaries – private, national, cultural – are no longer clearcut, and the state of nature thus emerges with a potentially conflictual wildness. Denying this is pointless and expecting to resolve it through the economy is an illusion. To equip each man and woman with a civil identity appropriate to their national identity seems the valid solution. An identity of this kind enables him or her to pass from the sphere of natural intimacy to that of civil life without alienating his or her own singulariy in one form or other of family as happened before, nor even in a neutral identity, which signifies a partial loss of identity.

In fact, the difficulties of coexistence between the sexes, between the generations, but also between races and cultures, arise because of a lack of civil protection of the individual, and because the various families which accommodated him/her took away his/her identity to form a relatively undifferentiated unity.

Constructing a European citizenship requires assuring the passage from natural to civil identity which presupposes taking certain differences into account in the construction of civil identity. This is clear, for example, as regards the sexes: a man has no need of the right to a free choice of maternity, despite the fact that a choice such as this is not without consequences for the individuals who love each other or for the two parents. Even between the generations, differences in the definition of civil identity impose themselves: rights and duties are not the same for an adolescent, an adult or an old person. Here, too, natural identity must become civil identity without eradicating its own properties or qualities. The same point could be made regarding the different cultural families: race, religion, belonging to a nation and even an ethnic grouping cannot be integrated into civil identity in the same way.

What seems obvious is the fact that coexistence in the community cannot be achieved without the protection of each of the individuals who make it up, by means of a specific civil identity for which s/he is responsible both with regard to her/himself and with regard to the community. A requirement of this kind is particularly essential in a multinational, multicultural and multiracial society like the European Union.

The importance of the family, whether in the narrow or the wider sense, has for a long time masked the need to establish civil rights for individuals. Rights relating to the possession of goods and property have prevailed, with relationships between individuals regulated, more often than not, by the penal and not the civil code. But the cohabitation of cultures, which is how we live now, does not tolerate leaving the role of arbitrator between individuals to the penal code because legislation of this sort does not augur well for peace and civil coexistence. Similarly, the coexistence of traditions cannot entrust customary law with its old function, because common laws vary and can conflict with each other, for example as regards marriage and guardianship but also inheritance, etc.

The construction of the European Union thus confronts us with the task of drawing up a new civil constitution. In this sense, it represents an opportunity in the process of History, an opportunity which should be grasped immediately for preserving human identity and for forestalling conflicts.

The draft code of citizenship which follows embraces this intention. It takes into account:
– the cohabitation of traditions and cultures;
– the necessary restructuring of the family and, therefore, of life as a couple also;
– the rights of young generations;
– the rights of the two sexes or genders;
– the problems which arise from the coexistence of various national codes and from the lack of any connection between these and the *Universal Declaration of Human Rights*.

The *Draft* lacks certain elements. But it offers an approach for reflection and communication both on European citizenship and on its relation to national citizenships, which ought also to be reconsidered.

Towards a Citizenship of the European Union

Draft Code of Citizenship
Luce Irigaray – Renzo Imbeni

Today we find ourselves forced to confront certain problems concerning civil society, and the relations between civil society and existing organizations of the State or of political parties: problems which call for a rethinking and redefinition of a fairer code of citizenship, one which is more in touch with reality.

Questions arise particularly regarding the status of individuals as civil individuals. Existing codes affirm as positive rights almost exclusively those relating to the ownership of goods. They have little to say about rights concerning the identity of individuals and the relationships between individuals as male and female citizens. Thus relations between individuals come to be considered and judged as a function of goods and often on the basis of penal law only. Legislation of this sort does not favour the structuring of a community based on the relationships between individuals.

Many factors moreover make it necessary in our times to define positive rights which guarantee a specific civil identity to male and female citizens.

– The coexistence of cultures, which necessitates a code of civil coexistence enabling various traditions, particularly religious ones, to live together.

– The coexistence of cultures, which poses anew the question of defining a specific individual identity.

Democracy Begins Between Two

— A relative destructuring of family unity, which requires that each man and woman should enjoy a specific civil identity which cannot be alienated in the family institution, a requirement which confirms the need for a new civil relationship between woman and man, women and men.

— An earlier attainment of civil maturity, which requires that young people be entrusted with specific civil responsibilities, in other words, that their identity receive real content.

— The organization of supranational community identities, which makes the redefinition of individual rights independent of nationality necessary, if one is to avoid the risk of falling back on nationalisms, fundamentalisms, racisms, etc.

— The current split between the content of national civil codes and constitutions and the *Universal Declaration of Human Rights* (it is not possible to apply the latter to other nations and cultures if one does not apply it to oneself).

— The divergences between the national civil codes of citizens summoned to live together in the sphere of vaster communal unities.

— The calling into practical, if not theoretical, question of certain aspects of democracy, which necessitates placing responsibility for themselves and for the community democratically back in the hands of male and female citizens. This would be equivalent to achieving true democracy for which appropriate civil rights are, as yet, lacking.

Towards a Citizenship of the European Union

— The lack of rights and responsibilities appropriate to real civil individuals: women and men. This deficiency is particularly obvious as regards women, which explains their recent emancipation from paternal or marital authority in the framework of the family institution.

The lack of legislation appropriate to women can be seen today in various ways: in particular, in the scandals and trials concerning the violence of which they are victims. National civil codes as well as constitutions, and the *Universal Declaration of Human Rights* all lack terms relating to specific rights which would enable such crimes to be judged. Thus rape is defined as a crime and not as rape, which fails to protect the woman as such and leaves the ordinary citizen unaware of the felony he commits when he rapes someone. The same is true as regards the free choice of maternity which is defined, at its best, as permission to have an abortion without penal consequences: such a formulation of the law reveals its complicity with patriarchal power which retains the right to legislate over a woman's body, even if she is of age. Women even lack rights relating to the custody of their children, especially in the case of intercultural marriages, rights relating to a culture appropriate to their identity (for example, rights prohibiting sexual mutilation), rights relating to their physical or symbolic representation in public places, etc. As long as such rights are lacking, crimes involving women are considered almost exclusively in the penal context which does not promote civil peace. What is more, no preventive legislation exists: one which would entrust a woman with responsibility for herself as a citizen and which, by considering her as a civil individual, would give the community the responsibility of preventing the crimes involving her, involving both of them.

Often clauses are added to civil codes, to constitutions and to the *Universal Declaration of Human Rights*, particularly at the request of women, which testify to the fact that the issues are not being dealt with exhaustively. On the other hand, when there is a clash of arguments, these are often expressed in too abstract and general a manner for each male and female citizen to be able to interpret and practise them. So law becomes a matter for experts in national and international jurisdiction. It no longer has the function of constituting and regulating a civil community made up of male and female citizens responsible for themselves and for the community. This lack is aggravated by the fact that legislation expresses itself in terms of the right to 'have', to satisfy needs and desires, to possess (including possession of one's own body understood as a good), rather than in terms of responsibility before oneself and before others as civil individuals.

The *Draft*, signed with both our names, was circulated in the European Parliament, distributed to various members either by Renzo Imbeni or by myself. We asked for opinions, critical responses, reactions. We also organized a meeting concerning this project in Brussels in the sphere of the European Parliament with about 25 members of parliament and 50 or so extraparliamentary political and cultural personalities present.

This initial *Draft* was taken up again insofar as was possible, given that the Treaty of Maastricht is what it is and the rules of the European Parliament are what they are, in the *Report* by Renzo Imbeni on European citizenship.

At this point in my account, the new possibilities and the fruitfulness of a task carried out jointly by a man and a woman are already clear. Of course, there were disagreements between us but, since both of us are fairly honest, we overcame the difficulties which were often only misunderstandings to be clarified or a collision between two different modes of political practice: one, more masculine, associated with a party politics, the other, more feminine, still outside any traditional institution.

THE REPORT OF RENZO IMBENI

I should like first and foremost to salute the effort which Renzo Imbeni has made to insert into his *Report* the most crucial material of the *Project*, almost half of which he has, moreover, quoted in the *Justification* of his *Proposal for Resolution*.

Democracy Begins Between Two

– Basing himself on article 8 of the Maastricht Treaty, he affirmed that citizenship of the Union offers a way towards the construction of a democratic politics at the level of the European community, because it entrusts male and female citizens of the member states with an active role within the community system (*Report*,[3] A, A).

– With this goal in mind, he emphasized the urgent need for 'the European entity to be politically organized and structured on the basis of a constitution as appropriate legislative framework for the definition of the rights and duties of the citizens of the Union' (*R.*, A, B).

– He mentioned that such rights and duties must 'develop the notion of citizenship and confer on it a dimension in keeping with the present structure of European society – multicultural, multi-ethnic and multireligious – which requires rules of coexistence founded on positive norms', something which would be in conformity with 'the political will in the making of the member states' (*R.*, A, C).

– He proposed that 'recognition of, and respect for, the difference between women and men' serve 'as the foundation of democratic union between citizens' with the aim of protecting and defending 'individual freedom' in a context of 'cultural plurality' (*R.*, A, D).

– He reaffirmed, in this respect, that 'community rights and duties will acquire value and effectiveness when one is able to refer to the principles of a Constitutional Charter of the Union' (*R.*, A, I) which will define citizenship 'in an autonomous manner based on the principles and on the politico-institutional arrangement set out by the future constitution' (R., A, J).

– This point is particularly decisive for the integration into the European Community of male and female citizens from other countries who reside within the territory of a member state, but for whom member states block the possibility of the European Community 'intervening to determine the conditions for acquiring, enjoying and losing such rights' (R., A, E). This forces the European Community to accept on its territory male and female citizens with respect to whom it has no right to legislate. This point is important for women as well since legislation in the member states varies in their regard, without mentioning the variations concerning customary law.

– He also explained the importance of constructing citizenship of the Union both 'in order to speed up the process of unifying and democratizing the community institutions' (R., A, K), and 'to make the right to work, to decent living conditions (minimum salary, health care, right to accommodation) and to protection of the environment fully effective' (R., A, L).

The proposals drawn up by Renzo Imbeni to be put to the vote by the European Parliament are thus defined with an eye to a general context which prevents them appearing as mere passwords, conferring on them instead a rational content which is bound up with the needs of our era, particularly those connected to coexistence in the community as far as differences are concerned.

They are thus defined on the basis of the same justifications, and sometimes in the same terms, as appear in the *Draft Code of Citizenship*. This in no way diminishes the political task accomplished by Renzo Imbeni. Quite the reverse! He tried to find a way of introducing the proposals of the *Draft* into the framework established by the Treaty of the European Union, an innovative task which can be shared by all men and women and which is not the preserve of arcane politicking. And it is a task which needed two people, carried out by listening to and respecting the thought and experience of a woman whose work is dedicated to trying to found a fairer future, particularly as regards relations between the sexes and between the genders.

Renzo Imbeni accepted that our paths would collide, one marked out on the basis of an ideal of equality for all men and women, the other from the necessity of respecting differences, and not negating them in the name of an equality defined in an abstract or purely economic fashion. So a man and a woman have been able to prove the fruitfulness of an alliance between the two genders operating in political theory and practice.

This is something new, still in its infancy, but drafting 'government as a couple' – if I can be allowed the expression – in this way highlights the historical impasses and the by now out-of-date nature of another type of politics.

However, we should not think of this as something

Towards a Citizenship of the European Union

which can easily be achieved every day. The faithfulness towards ourselves that both of us wanted to practise wounded us on more than one occasion, especially since faithfulness of this sort is connected with the historical past and with many people who sometimes do not understand the objective that we are trying to pursue. I must say that I do, in part, understand those politicians, male and female, who keep their work and emotional life strictly separate. I understand why they do so, but I believe that work like ours is indispensable if another stage in History is to be attained.

Renzo Imbeni's faithfulness to his own history can be seen in his *Report* and, in particular, in the points submitted to the vote by the European Parliament. For the most part, these are defined on the basis of his own experience: as secretary of the FGCI, as mayor of Bologna, as national executive of the PDS. He has placed this experience at the service of a definition of citizenship for the European Union.

This can be seen in the emphasis placed on the right 'to work, to parity of opportunity and to decent living conditions' (*R.*, A, 9, a) for all men and women, particularly for women, young people and foreigners from other countries.

But Renzo Imbeni's way of being democratic is not only formal nor limited to the economic field. He is concerned in particular with 'the right to information concerning the activities of the institution of the Union in order to guarantee its transparency and accessibility to citizens' (*R.*, A, 9, g). He also underlines the importance to be attributed to recourse to the Mediator : 'the right to have recourse to the Mediator, individually or by means of representative associations or with public juridical aid, even in the event of violation of fundamental rights and the possibility that the latter may have recourse to the Court of Justice' (*R.*, A, 9, h).

Renzo Imbeni, faithful to the tradition of the Italian Left and to its masters, is concerned to emphasize the 'right to enrich one's own culture and one's own training' (*D.R.*, A, 8, b) or the 'right of young people to study, culture and education' (*R.*, A, 9,b).

In keeping with his own party's programme and with the needs of our time, he asks for 'the right to a healthy environment and to respect for our health' (*R.*, A, 9, c), a request which is very dear to women, those who are already European or (we hope...) soon to become European, like the women of Norway or Sweden. Concern for the environment, for food and for health which are a consequence of it, ought to be one of the points which justify the European Union for these women, and I am in agreement with such a desire.

Another point on which Renzo Imbeni reveals that his attentiveness to democracy is not purely formal nor an empty slogan is the importance attributed to rights in his *Report*. It is impossible to speak of democracy in a community in which male and female citizens do not enjoy specific rights. Thus Renzo Imbeni's *Report* mentions the importance of the 'right to an active or passive vote in the European elections throughout the Union, irrespective of the member state of residence of the citizen' (*R.*, A, 9, f) and of the 'right of all professions to circulate freely and of all member states to have access to public office' (*R.*, A, 9, i). But he goes beyond this in demanding both the right to citizenship of the Union for residents of other countries: 'the right of residents of other countries, who regularly reside within the Union, to acquire, given specific conditions, citizenship of it' (*R.*, A, 9, j), and rights for women or, more precisely, sexed rights, for example 'the right of all, men and women, before the law to the juridical recognition of their identity as subjects of right, as the premise for an effective application of the principle of equality and of non-discrimination' (*R.*, A, 9, d). In the *Draft Report* this corresponds to the proposal 'the right to the juridical recognition of differences' – sexual amongst others – 'as the premise, etc.' (*D.R.*, A, 8, h).

On the last point, my intervention in the drawing up of the *Report* is obvious. And at the start it was not easy to convince a man of egalitarian persuasion like Renzo Imbeni of the necessity of sexed rights. I had to explain the reason for them, their historical usefulness, their democratic urgency. Once convinced, he became a better champion of women's rights in Parliament than many female members of parliament.

Perhaps the most telling trace of our joint work can be seen in the importance which Renzo Imbeni has given to the difference between ma(e)n and woma(e)n as condition of a democratic constitution of the Union.

In this respect, one finds in his *Draft Report* amongst the motives for the proposals submitted to the vote: 'maintaining that cultural plurality poses anew the problem of individual freedom and points to the requirement for respect for the difference between women and men as the foundation of democratic union between citizens, nations and cultures' (*D.R.*, A, E), to which motive the definitive *Report* adds the word 'recognition' '...the requirement for recognition and respect...'

One can only deplore the fact that the Commission for Women's Rights, in its own proposal for amendment, replaced the words '...respect for the difference between women and men...' (*D.R.*) with the words '...respect for individual choices...' In contrast to the formulation used in Renzo Imbeni's *Report*, this Commission tried to eradicate feminine identity and the man-woman difference, preferring the definition of a neutral individual.

The other amendments of the ex-C18 and the reasons given for them reveal the same tendencies. These amendments and reasons appear in its *Draft Opinion*.

THE OPINION OF THE COMMISSION FOR WOMEN'S RIGHTS

Already in October 1993 Renzo Imbeni had filed an official request, through the President of the European

Towards a Citizenship of the European Union

Parliament, with the Commission for Women's Rights for an opinion on his *Report*. It was not until 30 November that a reporter for the opinion was nominated: Mary Banotti, an Irish Catholic, a choice made based on rules requiring contrasting political opinions between reporter (male or female) and reporter of the opinion. At the same meeting on 30 November, the conclusions of a *Draft Opinion* were unanimously approved. Only the president (female), one of the vice-presidents (female), the reporter and seven women from the Commission, amongst whom were two replacements, were present.

In this *Draft Opinion:*
– It is correctly noted, as motive for the amendments, that women represent more than 50 per cent of the population of 'citizens' Europe' (1), but the fact that women's identity is different from men's, and therefore requires crucial innovations both in jurisprudence and culturally, is then deleted. Women, without 'discrimination', in other words without differences, are to be given the same rights as men (2).
– Citizenship is evoked as a 'concept' rather than as a concrete content appropriate to real persons. Each woman finds herself assimilated to a 'European citizen' [gram.masc.] whose status would be neutral from the point of view of gender (4).
– The need for collaboration between the European Parliament and national Parliaments is mentioned on 'a list of fundamental rights intended to come into effect

following the approval of national Parliaments', but the Commission for Women's Rights only communicates a draft list in somewhat abstract and general terms: 'right to equal opportunities' and 'all forms of discrimination against women are prohibited' (5).

– The emphasis is placed on the need for the European Union to embrace the 'concept' of 'full economic autonomy for women' as an element of the 'concept' of citizenship which would imply for women 'the status of economically independent citizens' (6). Although the terminology is sometimes questionable, the request expressed by this point of the *Opinion* is undoubtedly the strongest, most precise and most coherent, noting rigorously that 'women should enjoy the right to work, the right to dispose of their own goods, to obtain credit in their own name and the autonomous right to social security. Pension rights, especially, ought to be personal and ought not to depend on the contributions of third parties, which would enable them to be revoked in the event of divorce, separation or abandonment'.

– Next comes the reminder that parity requires 'making access to and participation in, the public and private institutions of our society equal' (7).

The most incisive words of the *Opinion* of the Commission thus relate to economic identity, an identity which is somehow neutral. In the final analysis, the request is for equality with men, and for obliterating one's belonging to an identity of one's own which might get in the way of it. In this sense I do not think that the Commission for Women's Rights represents the specific needs of all women, needs which are linked to their being women.

Of course, the position of the Women's Commission seems to pay attention to some of women's problems, but it cannot for this reason be said to be seeking new positive rights for them. Women's identity is outlined negatively, through what it lacks, the risks of discrimination linked to gender, the economic difficulties lived by women. The request is above all to be recognized as a 'citizen' [gram. masc.] on an equal footing. But there is no statement nor question concerning who woman is and what her needs are. Even the emphasis placed on the social dimension, with a certain contempt for the civil, intensifies this obliteration of an identity specific to woman.

I even find myself asking: how are the female members of parliament on this Commission to be defined as women? Is it purely a question of a biological identity? This is not enough to ensure representation for either sex, especially if the dimension of sexed civil identity is denied. To be born a woman should not be sufficient grounds for claiming to represent the rights of women, without a code of rights which ensures an objective mediation between the woman who represents and the women represented. It is dangerous to govern in the name of the state of nature! And, in my view, the claims of social justice are not enough to justify a separate Commission for women: woman as woman is not yet defined on it as a civil individual, and the conflicts between women are not arbitrated by it in the name of civic-mindedness and even less of women's civilization. To say that it is enough to be elected opens the way, in addition, to various forms of abuse and violence which cannot be regulated through the social dimension alone. It is a question of the civil level, as it is the task of the civil level to ensure coexistence between men and women.

I fear that a separate Commission for Women's Rights, which does not involve itself as a priority in the dimension of civil identity, may become a space reserved for female claims in the context of a Parliament which will simply ignore women's problems, leaving them as the responsibility of the Commission reserved for them. This is serious because it risks making the current necessities of the feminine world appear through a screen which, in my view, is neither adequate nor appropriate on decisive points.

Now the Parliament is already addressing requests sent by a woman for women to this Commission. I will give you an example of this. On the occasion of my meeting on 10 November 1993 at the European Parliament, I had prepared a petition-letter, addressed to the President of the Parliament, requesting rights for adult women and girls, rights appropriate to the multicultural character of the European Union.

Towards a Citizenship of the European Union

To the President of the European Parliament
Egon Klepsch

Brussels, 10 November 1993

Dear Mr President,
I'm writing to you on the occasion of the ratification of the Treaty of Maastricht, spurred on by certain articles of this treaty concerning European citizenship and, also, by the possibility that each citizen, male and female, has of addressing a petition to Parliament in their own name.

I am not going to use this petition simply as a means of calling for justice: denunciation in a matter like this has existed in many forms and for some years. But to found a new community on countless trials is neither desirable nor even possible.

My request therefore concerns a preventive measure for the democratic functioning of the Union, particularly in its multicultural dimension.

I am asking for the 'recognition', by means of a European Constitution, of the 'physical and moral inviolability of woman as woman'.

I am asking that this inviolability be guaranteed by means of written rights for which the Union stands guarantor, rights which would entrust each female citizen who is of age with the juridical responsibility for her body and her word, in the sphere of both public and private life.

For minors, I am asking that parental custody be constitutionally backed up with custody by the Union (guaranteed by written laws and exercised, in the event of controversy, by the guardianship of a couple) which would protect children, and especially girl children, from the possibility of sexual abuse, and that this would continue until they came of age juridically.

I remain at the disposal of the European Parliament for defining (with the help of a research group made up, amongst others, of lawyers) and presenting to its attention a charter of the specific rights necessary for the recognition of the civil identity of woman as woman, whether she is of age or not.

I look forward to hearing from you,

Yours faithfully,

Luce Irigaray
Director of Research in Philosophy at the CNRS

Those who wish to sign should add their name and surname in block letters, their signature and, if possible, their address and profession.

Towards a Citizenship of the European Union

After the reading of the letter, I had it signed by those present and, subsequently, by people in some of the countries I had visited: France and Italy, for example. The letter is still circulating today in France, Italy, Spain, Germany ... I sent an initial copy to Egon Klepsch, through Renzo Imbeni and Brigitte Ernst de la Graete, members of the European Parliament, in December. After waiting a long time, I heard in May, thanks to a missive from Rosi Bindi, who heads the Commission for Petitions, that the terms of the letter are appropriate to the Treaty of Maastricht and that, given the relevance of the requests, it would be passed on to the Commission for Women's Rights for an opinion. Now, so far, this Commission has not been in favour of rights for women as women from fear of affirming their difference. Sometimes it is more backward-looking on certain points than individual, commonsense men and women. What will the Commission make of a request of this sort? I hope, with the opening of the new parliamentary season, to receive an opinion, and that the women of the Women's Commission will invite me to discuss this topic.

I pushed very hard last year for this dialogue with a result that, in my view, was not positive enough, except perhaps for the presence of a significant number of women members of parliament at the meeting of 10 November 1993 and at the vote in the chamber of 19 January 1994.

– I have seen to it personally that all the women on the Commission for Women's Rights received the *Draft*

Code of Citizenship accompanied by a letter. I did this in September, at the opening of the new parliamentary season. I received a reply from only two members of parliament, Brigitte Ernst de la Graete and Birgit Cramon Daiber, who expressed their interest in working with me.

– I spoke on the telephone with many women – and even men – from various groups and commissions, in accordance with the practice of transversality used in the politics of women's liberation in relation to already existing parties, groupings and institutions. (In this respect, I have to say that the warmest welcome often came from the Greens.) So I did my share of preparing for the 10 November meeting in Brussels so far as my involvement went, while Renzo Imbeni was establishing contacts in Parliament itself.

– At the time of this meeting, I tried to get female and male members of the European Parliament to engage in a dialogue with national members of parliament and extraparliamentary political and cultural personalities. I also invited to it people that I knew, who were involved in social work with prisoners, women from the Third World, mothers whose children have been taken from them, women who have been raped or who are facing problems in their marriage, people belonging to political and religious groups, etc.

– I tried to establish contacts between women that I knew and the (female) member of parliament for their country or region.

– More recently, I went to see the women's repre-

Towards a Citizenship of the European Union

sentative in Norway, Britt Foegner, to try and coordinate our action concerning new rights for women and the Norwegian women's objections to their country's entry into the European Union. Having met several groups of them, I can already say that they are afraid of losing the advantages that have been gained, of being subjected to pollution of the natural environment and of food, that respect for the cultivation of the earth and its products will be forgotten (for example, that farms will be bought up for tourism, with no obligation to ensure the cultivation of their lands).

So I tried hard to establish a dialogue with women, particularly, but not only, with the women of the Commission for Women's Rights. Renzo Imbeni did the same in the context of his work. The results have not been what we, or at least I, hoped for, neither on the level of reciprocity of words, nor as far as the content of the *Opinion* of the Women's Commission is concerned.

Thus, I wonder why the reporter for the *Opinion* did not pass on to the Commission for Public Freedom and Internal Affairs additional amendments concerning all the forms of violence to which women are subjected, the free choice of one's sexuality or of maternity, specific working hours, the necessity of a sexed culture, the custody of children in the event of separation, divorce or intercultural marriages. The women of the ex-C18 had the possibility of doing this, given the presentation of Renzo Imbeni's *Report*. But, unlike the latter, they

Democracy Begins Between Two

contented themselves with a request for equality which does not bring out women's specific needs nor how to resolve the conflicts between men and women. They also neglected respect for difference between the genders as a possible way towards coexistence between all the other forms of difference.

They address claims to men in the name of women but do not propose a two-gender citizenship which, by respecting the man-woman difference, would protect a democratic Union founded in diversity. Indeed, they do not seem to have any positive model of living together to propose, either for women or between men and women.

Now this dimension of civilization is somewhat feminine, and it is not desirable that it should be obliterated in the conquest of equality with men.

One sometimes hears it said that patience is needed as far as women's search for a politics of their own is concerned, and I tell myself this almost everyday. But I also note that the democratic tendencies of women's liberation are in some ways a step behind us, and this causes me concern both on behalf of all women, and of society as a whole.

I do not believe that the surest way now towards democracy is for women to wish to equal men. And the current repression of Marxism risks submerging voices in feminine mode of this kind.

I think that it is rather in terms of difference that we should be seeking equivalence and equality of rights today. In his *Report*, Renzo Imbeni insisted more than once on the importance of respecting differences. I have already given an example of this concerning the foundation of democracy. Apart from the importance of the 'recognition of differences and respect for the difference between men and women' as the basis for democratic union between everyone, men and women, Renzo Imbeni asks, as I have already mentioned, for the 'juridical recognition of differences', including sexual ones, 'as the premise for the effective application of the principle of non-discrimination and equality of all before the law'. Yet again, the Women's Commission amended the proposal in the direction of neutrality and abstraction: erasing the word difference and replacing it with the expression 'subjects of right', with the subsequent addition: 'men and women, in their capacity as male and female citizens'. It seems to me that the Women's Commission, by speaking of subjects of right in their capacity as male and female citizens, tried to obliterate the fact that such subjects ought to be recognized as juridically distinct.

TOWARDS A CITIZENSHIP OF THE UNION?

Matters were not straightforward within the European Parliament either, particularly in Commission 14, which deals with public freedom and to which Renzo Imbeni belonged. His report, of the utmost rigour and quality, did not please all men nor all women. Perhaps for this

Democracy Begins Between Two

very reason! Usually neither male nor female politicians take enough time to think, to weigh things up, to plan and build a future.

I'll give you a few examples of the difficulties encountered. A French right-wing member of parliament, even though he considered Renzo Imbeni a likeable and tolerant man, was furiously opposed to the idea that a supranational legislation might change national customs and rights. A German female member of parliament refused to grasp that the proposal 'free choice of maternity' is not the same as a papal repression of abortion. A Belgian socialist member, who does not want to know anything about a European civil code, also comes to mind, not to mention the English member of parliament who does not even know what a national civil code means. Or the female member of parliament who, affirming herself as a woman, fears the loss of her rights as a 'citizen' [gram. masc.]; or another, who cannot bear hearing about anything unless it has contributed to her liberation or relates to her subjective experience.

I shall stop here, but I am not forgetting all the absent members of parliament, those who are so busy piling up terms of office that they never have time, those who conduct their campaigns in their own backyards, those who would rather get involved in publicity scoops than with serious objectives. What is more, there was little time for effective discussion and the number of languages spoken made dialogue difficult.

So it was hard work to obtain 13 votes in favour as opposed to 9 against in the debate in Commission 14.

During this debate an opinion was sought both from the Commission for Women's Rights and from the Institutional Commission. The latter voted in favour of Renzo Imbeni's *Report*.

As already mentioned, the Commission for Women's Rights did not do much concerning the opinion sought both by me and by Renzo Imbeni on the topic of a new European citizenship; it did not talk much with us. This strikes me as an error that should not be repeated: the content of our proposals was, and will remain, in favour of individuals and particularly of women.

In conclusion, it is with great sadness, both personally and politically, subjectively and objectively, that I note that Renzo Imbeni's *Report* was not approved this time by the European Parliament. How are we to make sense of this? Many women, many men, were amazed at it. I'll suggest several motives. To begin with, Renzo Imbeni's *Report* was innovative, but we cannot avoid innovating as far as Europe is concerned since it is something new to be built. Next, the right and the extreme right were opposed, either proposing that the Commission adjourn or imposing last minute amendments in the chamber which were unacceptable to Renzo Imbeni; as a result, he asked for a vote against his *Report*, thus amended.

In addition, left-wing members did not pay enough attention to the importance of proposals for a future society which could be lived and shared by all men and all women. Votes that were needed to obtain decisive rights for male and female citizens were lacking as, for example, four concerning the proposal that a European Constitution should entrust women in private and public life with greater civil autonomy and responsibility thus overcoming 'the residual juridical norms of patriarchal stamp still current in the legislations of many member states' (*R*., A. 10). Votes were lacking because the interested male or female members of parliament did not pay enough attention, were not present.

This should not happen again, on pain of handing one's vote to the right or the extreme right. We are dealing here quite simply with reality: if you are not present at a vote, you are cancelling your vote, your choice, and allowing in another tendency which will lay down the law to you.

This is reality, and my account is an accurate reflection of it.

I hope that it can serve as a lesson for the present and the future.

Refounding the Family on a Civil Basis

I am often reproached for asking so much of women. It is true that I expect a great deal, especially of myself and so, too, of all women. This is because I believe that women can open up a new era in History, in other words a possible future for humanity. So I am constantly asking them not to fall asleep, to remain awake so that they can behave in an attentive and coherent way to be sure of accomplishing the historical task that is theirs.

This is certainly not a negligible task and women, we women, only recently awakened to a subjectivity of our own, find ourselves shouldering a historical responsibility which does not always leave us time to savour the first fruits of our liberation. Especially since some men can even be heard nowadays talking about their feminine selves, their feminine kind of pleasure, at the very moment that we women are busy disinterring the traces of our subjectivity, caught up

---

Talk given at the National Conference of Women of the PDS (Rome, 12 December 1993).

Democracy Begins Between Two

in the laborious process of constructing our own identity.

But that is how it is. And the important thing really, I feel, is to know what is to be done and how to do what is necessary to guarantee the existence of a world that is livable in the future, livable in a way that, hopefully, is more human, happier, that is less prey to the instinct to dominate and to possess the other, above all the other sex, the other gender.

This form of domination is often exercized by men over women but also, in another form, by women over their children. Even if the ways in which it operates and their effects are different, this double form of domination does exist, and one form can explain the other: the woman, subjected to the husband, transmits her alienated state to her son, and the son to his wife. So we are caught up in a vicious circle with no way out. The alienation which exists between the genders is, as those early militants of the 1960s and 1970s claimed, born of difference and has to be dealt with from a basis in difference. If we are to be liberated from this alienation, the way in which both the genealogical relation between the genders, and the horizontal one between men and women, is lived, has to be transformed.

So it is no longer solely a question of our own liberation but of that of the couple, and that of the family in both the narrow and wider sense: political family, cultural family, religious family, for example.

Unless the laws and customs which still organize all

Refounding the Family on a Civil Basis

forms of the family today are transformed, the liberation of humanity, of which women's liberation forms a determining part in our times, cannot occur.

Indeed, in the sphere of the family, there are still traces of an animality which cannot safeguard our emergence into a fully human freedom and responsibility.

But it may be that nowadays the things that come to us from furthest away oblige us to resolve what is closest, in other words, what is hardest to see, to understand and to change: habits and customs. The fact that there are now families, in both the narrow or wider sense, made up not only of different sexes, but also of different races and cultures, forces us to rethink and to modify our way of living. This is true of Italy; and will be even more true in the future because of Europe.

So, as men and women, we have to protect the form of alliance that the family offers not by regressing to a state of natural unity, an instinctual contract or an emotional pact, but by taking a step forward towards winning a civil identity for ourselves, as human individuals.

In fact, I think that most of the violence that occurs in cities, between cities, countries, ethnic groups and cultures has a common origin in the lack of civil relationships within the family itself.

We have to protect peace and civil coexistence first and foremost in the home; a more civil form of behaviour outside will follow automatically.

Democracy Begins Between Two

The most pressing task today, particularly for women, is to work towards refounding the family on the basis of civil coexistence. It is indispensable for their liberation, and indispensable if we are to move into an enlarged community like Europe, since the only valid counterweight to reducing Europe to one huge market is to protect human identity. This human identity is, first and foremost, an identity linked to the family. As such it has, until now, remained a natural form of identity linked to unconscious habits; we have to transform it into a civil identity.

This may not seem much. But, in fact, it represents a decisive gesture in the face of all forms of power and of war.

I think that today it is more useful, and indeed indispensable as I've already argued, to deal with things where they arise, starting from their foundation, as it were. Now the basis of the civil community is not one + one + one ... more or less neutral individuals; it is the family. The women who were behind the gains made by the women's liberation movement know all too well that the private is political; and that, if the State wants to close its eyes and pretend that it knows nothing about what is going on in the home, that is because it suits it very well if things stay the way they are.

It is both disheartening yet amusing to observe how many people feel that the family must not be interfered with. But, in fact, the State already interferes in it: by

Refounding the Family on a Civil Basis

levying taxes, wanting children, accepting that instinctual violence should be on public display, and promoting families who help to develop the national heritage.

The family therefore – whether in its narrow or wider sphere – has to be refounded on the basis of civil relations between woman and man, women and men, and also between parents and children.

Up until now the protection of relations within the family has been religious rather than civil. Developing the history of humanity means protecting relations within the family with civil rights, and leaving an individual's choice of religion free. A step of this kind implies making civil coexistence a coexistence which encompasses a certain religious element, but of a civil nature and not in the sense of belonging to a religious family. If we are to accede to this stage in our historical development, we have to leave childhood, dependence and irresponsibility behind. We have to be capable of our own self-government, of representing ourselves in a civil way as women.

Our alienation derives essentially from our being reduced to the natural state, to a nature-body capable of reproducing, for example, but also to an identity which is solely instinctive, emotional, tied to this nature-body.

If we are to emerge from this alienation it is up to us, as women, to make the move from natural to civil identity. Nobody can do this for us. And we have to ask those who are preventing us from doing so, for the rights associated with the recognition of a civil identity appropriate to our natural identity: the right to the free choice of maternity, the right to the dignity of a civil individual, the right to a culture appropriate to us, etc.

Without rights which are suited to our feminine gender, we will continue endlessly to fall back under nature's domination, whether this is imposed by husband, State or Church, or by our own subjectivity which lacks the necessary boundaries for ensuring the return to the self and for organizing coexistence with others.

It seems to me that this need for women of today to enjoy a form of civil self-representation before representing other women or men, is also a requirement of a democratic ideal. I am not sure that we should retain the word 'democracy', power of the people. It would be better, I believe, to discover a new term which would guarantee to all wo/men rights which would not alienate the rights of each wo/man. I am searching for this new word as I am speaking about civil rights appropriate to real people, their gender included.

Representing our singularity in this way, which can be extended to embrace our gender as far as the civil community is concerned, is, in my view, indispensable, if we are to establish a civil, democratic society on a new basis.

What we are talking about here is the impossibility of representing an individual, male or female, without the mediation afforded by appropriate rights. Political

Refounding the Family on a Civil Basis

representation then takes place in the name of a right which is common to the person who represents and to the person represented; and whoever governs is simply the woman or man who sees to the application of the law. The person who governs does not enjoy arbitrary power, not even a form of power or a mandate linked with her/his nature since this would constitute a danger politically. S/he is in the service of the application of the civil self-representation of each person, male or female.

In this way, we women have to pass through the civil community before thinking about mechanisms for political representation.

Our liberation therefore encompasses the liberation of the family in the narrow sense and of all forms of civil community.

I hope, we hope, that women will not retreat in the face of such a task. The women who gave birth to the women's movement in the 1960s and 1970s were always aware that we women are alienated because of our nature and that, in order to escape this alienation, we have to have rights which protect this difference.

We were aware of this, together we willed it, women of all ages, classes, races and colours, and we obtained the beginnings of a change in the civil code despite the existing legislation, despite the male majority in Parliament.

We obtained it because we stood together, all women as one, each woman growing through the recognition and growth of every other woman. All that we asked for at that point was the right to civil representation for each woman.

We hope that now, a little richer, a little more visible, women will not forget each individual woman, near or far, great or small, in this country or some other; that we will fight the battle together for each woman. And that it will not be fought only for a few who hope to feather their own nests, losing sight of the historical task which falls to all of us.

This task, which is ours through historical necessity, also represents what should today favour an alliance between those men and women who seek a form of politics which will guarantee each individual's right to his or her singularity: progressive Catholics, for example, but also the militants of 1968, the Greens, the militants on the Left who are concerned about more than just economic problems.

Paying attention in this manner to the rights of the individual seems to me also a way of entrusting each man and woman with personal responsibility, and with a means of resistance in the face of danger of a fascist sort.

I shall take the liberty of reminding those who are not fond of legislation that the oppressed, the enslaved, the exiles, all those who have been wounded in some sense, desire to be protected by legislation and ask especially for their right to exist to be guaranteed.

To the rich, this necessity seems out of date; if they

Refounding the Family on a Civil Basis

appeal to the law, it is to protect their possessions a little more securely. The poor, however, make their appeal for the recognition of their very existence, their very identity.

To demand the right to at least a human identity for each man and woman seems to me, in the current economic crisis, more than ever necessary. According to the laws which at present govern us, men and women who do not have work, who do not have any possessions, count for nothing. It seems to me indispensable that they should at least retain their status as civil persons, recognized as such, and that they should not be subjected to a paternalism that strips them of their dignity as human beings.

On this point, the essential requirements of women are entirely similar to those of people who have nothing.

After all, placing the emphasis on the civil recognition of the individual in his/her singularity offers a way of escaping the domination of one individual by another.

So a man's value, as a civil person, is no greater than a woman's. The values are different, and this difference, protected by civilization, permits a relationship of reciprocity between them.

This is not easy perhaps, but nor is domination or conflict: they remain within the slave-master framework inspite of some overturning.

Reciprocity refuses this game between two, who remain two poles of a unique subject. Reciprocity obliges each woman and each man to remain within the self and to respect that s/he is irreducible, as is the other. This provides another way of emerging from childhood and dependence.

It is also a question of encouraging the idea that the purpose of sexual difference is not only the production of children but also of energy, creativity, happiness. Woman and man could then help each other to remain faithful to themselves, and to share and cultivate with the other an excess which is linked to their own relation as two.

I could say much more on this topic, and also about the idea that, if we are to escape from all forms of authoritarianism, it would be better to imagine government by a couple rather than by a man or a woman who, however well-intentioned, produce certain effects of power. For today I shall leave open this perspective of a change in the family which would extend from the most private aspect of our individual existence to the most political aspect of our life as a community.

A final word: I have chosen to speak of the family in the ordinary sense of the term. It seemed to me that this topic could serve as a point of departure for defining a woman's politics in a progressive political family.

But I should also like to make it clear that the need to define rights which are appropriate to sexed existence concerns all women.

Asking for the right to civil identity does not imply

preferring one sexual choice to another. It comes first. The right to enjoy a civil identity does not entail a duty to make this or that emotional choice. Instead, it represents a new achievement for each woman. The battle for the passage from the state of nature to civil identity can be fought by all women together, without any risk of failing to respect each individual woman.

For this reason, it strikes me as a valid project or programme, in addition to the fact that a right to be oneself as a woman corresponds to a contemporary need. We need a transportable home in which we can find ourselves wherever we are, in spite of the multiple directions which, in everyday life, lure us ever further from ourselves.

Democracy is Love

It was not long ago, I have to admit, that I began reading the work of Enrico Berlinguer. I am reading it with joy and surprise because, on many points, I feel close to him. As well as making me happy, this strengthens me in my intuitions or ideas, and allows me to draw closer to you without losing contact with myself.

Why has it taken me so long to discover Enrico Berlinguer's work? The main reason is that it has not been translated into French. Today, this seems to me a historical scandal and, as one who has never done any translation – except of my own work, for example of *To Be Two*, – I should like to make a part of Enrico Berlinguer's work known to the French-speaking public.

So I want to start with some words of his which cheered me up and which seem to me promising insofar as the possibility of realizing your ideals, particularly those of the young, is concerned. I quote first from a speech made in 1955.

Talk given at the Festival of Unity at the invitation of Young Left (Imola, 15 July 1994).

Democracy is Love

We would never be revolutionaries if we did not appreciate life, if, like monks, we thought of the world as a vale of tears, and that we are born to suffer ... If life for so many nowadays is a vale of tears, we know – and this is what we are fighting for – that it can become a vale no longer of tears, but of joy, flowers and smiling faces for everyone. This is precisely why we are communists, and why we are fighting so that everyone can savour the joys of life and, amongst these, the joys of love. (...) There are young communists who are ready to call out the password of women's liberation, arguing that women's social position must be equal to men's, but who then, in practice, behave towards their own girlfriends as though they were inferior beings and look on and treat them as such.

Berlinguer had understood that emancipation of women on a social level is not enough, and that we have to pursue such a task of human liberation into the life of the emotions, into our love life. In this way, through a more emotional and physical relationship, it could escape the exploitation of the other, male or female, avoid reducing them to being an object at one's disposal or a means of production, whether of manpower or of children.

I imagine that you are familiar with these words which I have only just discovered. And you will certainly recognize those of Marx: 'No man who oppresses a woman can be free'. It was actually a man, of the

Federation of Bologna, who quoted them to me five years ago. But words like these have not yet been understood, and it is worth reflecting on them once again and putting them into practice.

I, a woman who is part of women's liberation, am all too aware that the private is, as we say, political, and that democracy begins in the intimacy of love and of the home. Enrico Berlinguer was not afraid to speak of love, inspite of his status as a political leader. He was right in this and I salute his courage. I quote him again:

> The attitude of young communist men and women as regards the problems that love poses, is serious, aware, honest. We have no desire to train them as monks; we want young people to enjoy all the beauty and joy of life, of which love in all its fullness is a part.

We should not renounce love but educate it so that we can be faithful, even in passion, to our highest ideal. Let us leave scorn of the flesh to monks, as Berlinguer recommends – it would have been more accurate, in my view, to say priests, since monks are a bit different. Sanctifying love does not mean that we have to look on the flesh as sinful, but that it has to be transformed, transfigured, through love itself.

But how is this to be done? Which is the path that leads to love and happiness as two beings, including the carnal level? I have dedicated myself to this task for 20 years and I was comforted to find in Enrico Berlinguer

Democracy is Love

a recognition of the political importance of such work. I should add that your invitation and the presence of Renzo Imbeni have a similar meaning for me. And I thank you also for your recognition.

Work like mine, I must say, brings with it the joys that accompany a task dedicated to the liberation of humanity, but it also entails the difficulties and criticism associated with a real political commitment. It is true that I have learnt, in this respect, to measure the importance of something by the extent to which it is rejected, or by the degree of opposition that it encounters.

But we are gathered here in the name, rather, of happiness. And I hope that you will permit me to read some more of Enrico Berlinguer's words as a dedication to what I have said on *To Be Two*. They come from an introduction to an anthology for young communist women published in 1949.

> It is absolutely not our intention to deny young women the right to choose what they read, to be stirred by adventures or love stories. All we want to do is to help them understand that, sometimes, the aim of the author of these adventures or of the person who imagines these love stories, is to provide us with a vicarious involvement in adventures which are not ours, to make us dream of things that are not part of our world so that we are prevented from opening our eyes, from joining forces, from acting together to remove the obstacles that prevent so many

young women from building a future for themselves, living their own dream of love to fulfilment, having, all of them, their own families and achieving their own happiness in a society which would no longer know, as is the case for a few, privilege, luxury, caprice and, for many, humiliation, mockery and suffering.

We want, above all, to point out to young women that other books have been written, that other types of reading material exist, material which can, also, reflect their dreams and their aspirations, which can also be thrilling, because it speaks of the greatest of all adventures, our everyday life.

This, I think, is the sense in which I am proposing *To Be Two* and *I Love To You* for you to read. They have been written, partly, with you in mind, to leave a few pebbles, a few stars along your path so that you can walk it more easily. Even though these books are sometimes hard to read, since they have been written with sensitivity, I believe that they can awaken your attention, your heart, your spirit. I am sure that, comforted as I now am by the words of Enrico Berlinguer, I will be better able to address you in the future.

The Prologue to *To Be Two* presents some episodes of a rebirth from nature, one which takes place in spring, the time of the rebirth of the cosmos itself. Personally, I feel that to be born again from nature is definitely necessary for us to be able, at least once, to experience the acquisition of an autonomy that is neither aggressive nor violent; and we should develop ourselves each day out of loyalty to this sort of experience.

But, as the book goes on to say, 'Hardly is she reborn from it than he arrives'.

And, from then on, things become a bit more complicated. I have not said less pleasant, though, simply more complex. Pursuing a path opened up in *I Love To You* along more physical, sensory lines, I wonder how a relationship as two can be practised without being reduced to the desire to appropriate and to consume, but involving, on the contrary, an ability to relate to the self in order to perceive and contemplate who the other is, and also to be able to feel oneself as oneself, female or male, as well as the attraction to the other, male or female.

So there is a rhythmic pulse which beats between going out towards the other and returning to the self, between extending oneself as far as the other and returning to dwell within the self, between coming out into the light and going back into the darkness, into the invisibility of interiority, into the mystery of alterity.

This movement resembles that of the heart, of the circulation of blood, but also that of the cosmos itself which exists between expansion and concentration. It is true of the entire universe, but can already be seen in the sap of the plant world, in the behaviour of animals, just as in the movement of the sea, in the alternating of the seasons, in the respective intensities of the light and of the heat of the sun, in the cycles of humidity and dryness, of the winds, of the cyclones.

But there is a further problem between us, man and woman: we are two. How is this two to be articulated in the relationship with these natural rhythms? The question is so difficult that many different solutions have been imagined as a way of avoiding it. The being-two is, after all, only one (this is sometimes true but is not desirable in the long run, for example, in the family); one (female) is receptive and fertile nature and the other (male) the active labourer who carries the seed; or, a further possibility, one (female) is the mother of the son and the other (male) father of the daughter, in a relation of physical love also. What has not yet been imagined in thought is: how to remain together while still being two, how to be and become subjectively two, how to discover a way of coexisting as two beings, private and public, a way of living and thinking and loving as two beings without one being reduced to the other?

Perhaps it is possible for me, thanks to the respect that I feel for the other as other, to articulate both attraction and restraint with respect to him. I go out from and return to myself in order to respect his alterity, and this respect for the other becomes respect for myself, my life and my growth. So there is no longer fusion or submission, but the existence of a two which is irreducible to one or to the simple opposition between one (male) and the other (female), a reduction which makes them simply two poles of the one.

I have learnt another way from my own experience and from the traditions of the Far East, in particular from the most primitive Indian cultures, the most local and female ones, which are more mystical and less ritualistic, less magical than the male cultures which come after. These primitive cultures practise the differences in the relationship between man and woman, including in physical love. But, for them, it is not a question of a dual polarity within the one, as things still are in the West where, from Aristotle onwards, it is said that man is hot, dry, active and woman, in contrast, damp, cold and passive. They talk instead of drawing out the qualities of the one (female) and the other (male). So, for example, in the East, woman is referred to as hot inside and cold outside, man as cold inside and hot outside. In this case, respecting the difference makes desire for the other possible without having to renounce the self. The woman desires the heat in the man which enables her to return to the heat in herself.

Perhaps it is not easy to respect these differences. The qualities of the one (male) or the other (female) seem similar, able to be adapted to the one (female) or the other (male). Today it is often claimed that there are no insuperable differences between man and woman.

What is forgotten, in this case, is that difference is the source of desire and pleasure, and that remaining in

Democracy Begins Between Two

a relation of resemblance implies staying on a superficial level – one that is inevitably conflictual, according to Sartre, as I mention in *To Be Two*, – that fails, for example, to connect the heat that lies deep within the woman with the cold that is her more superficial element. The nostalgia for the heat leads the woman to seek the relation with the mother. This play between surface and depth can, on the contrary, be realized between the two genders given the difference between man and woman, not only in the contrast between hot and cold but also between low and high tones and between colours: red and blue, for example.

Respect for sexual difference, moreover, creates a framework which throws more clearly into relief the individual differences of each man and woman. Since I respect the other as other, irreducible to myself, I see him, listen to him and perceive him better in the detail of his particularity. In *To Be Two*, I spend quite a bit of time on this way of drawing close to the other. I speak of the way of perceiving the other, of seeing him and listening to him, and I try to define a way of touching him, of caressing him, so that neither the *I* nor the *thou* is lost, searching in this way for a relation between two which respects identities made up of different bodies and words.

In fact, a new relationship with the other provides, as well as the return to nature, the means of reconciling the cosmos and the world created by man in the direction of a new way, a new style of doing and

Democracy is Love

creating, which can more easily be shared by man and woman.

Here again the culture of the Far East has helped me: the story of the Buddha, for example, who seeks enlightenment sitting under a tree or contemplating a flower, but also in the patient practice of yoga or in the reading of some of the texts of this tradition. I have discovered in this way that it is possible to integrate the micro with the macrocosm, the nature inside me with that which surrounds me, and that it is possible to communicate with the other thanks to this knowledge.

This culture has taught me to perceive rather than simply to experience through the senses; and it is perception that opens up the possibility of a relationship between two in a way that sensation does not allow. The latter often entails a reduction of two subjects to two opposing modes of one and the same type of being, active or passive, for example. So the man becomes the one who provides pleasure and the woman the one who experiences it.

Therefore, in order to rediscover or to uncover man's being or that of woman, it appears necessary to leave behind the mode of experiencing which is limited to sensation, one that moreover complements our abstract manner of understanding, and to accede to a culture of the senses in which sensibility and thought come together.

If I had used sensation only, I would not have been able to write either *To Be Two* or *I Love To You*. What I have done, rather, is to practise perception and concentration on what is perceived. Instead of merging the perceived [gram. masc.] and perceiving [gram. fem.] into one, I tried on the contrary, to distinguish the perceived from the perceiving, to distinguish the *thou* from the *I* in order to safeguard the two. I did not make the perceived mine, but meditated on the revelation of the other which was thus uncovered, in order to return it to its own being rather than to appropriate it as mine.

It is not, then, a question of remaining at the level of unmediated experience, of my unmediated sensing of the other, but of stopping in front of a perception of this kind and, instead of simply pronouncing 'it is mine', of saying 'it is born from two and belongs to two'.

Probably because I am a woman, the goal of my path is to cultivate the relation between two subjects, to seek along the way spiritual awareness, happiness and a dwelling in the self, the instasy, rather than the ecstasy that is accomplished in transcending the subject-object split, which is a more masculine ideal.

This partly explains why we have to maintain a verbal exchange with the other: what I have perceived through him, I thus return to him. I reveal to him a part of his being which has revealed itself to me, and I invite him to inhabit his own being in a better way. I try in this way to become of assistance to him, while all the while respecting what is mysterious in him, the invisibility of his interiority. But, simultaneously, my words are an appeal addressed to him. I am saying to the other that his being and my being have, in some

Democracy is Love

sense, encountered each other. I'm calling on him to be attentive to what I have perceived, heeded, received from him, and to give value to the truth which is thus announced to him. I am asking him to respond from his truth and from that of the being revealed to him by me.

This is not, then, an affection which seduces the other into renouncing the intellect and the spirit, falling back into unmediated sensibility, but instead a determination to lead the lived experience of the sensibility towards coexisting with the other, thanks to a measure of respect, rationality and thought.

To Be Two, like *I Love To You*, bears witness to my desire to develop a culture of being-two, a culture of intersubjectivity.

Defining this most recent work of mine as 'focusing on the intimate' seems to me to perpetuate the split between private and public spheres of life, a split which forms the basis of our patriarchal type of society. This has led both to the subjection of woman to the father and the husband, and to the development, in woman, of an immature feminine subjectivity and to a consequent over-emphasis on the maternal instinct.

What I am trying then to do, in faithfulness to the work I have dedicated to the liberation of women, and first and foremost to my own liberation, is to define a relationship between two within sexual difference which is able to overcome the flaws and lacks characteristic of such a relationship in our History thus far.

Democracy Begins Between Two

A task of this sort, as I already indicated at the time of the publication of *I Love To You*, is a political one in the service of democracy. A real democracy must take as its basis, today, a just relationship between man and woman. A distorted relationship between them gives rise to many forms of antidemocratic power. Unless we can transform this, the most everyday element of our lives, we will never bring about change across the world.

Indeed, society is not made up of one + one + one neutral and separate individuals, but of individuals who are linked together, particularly through sexed relationships. In founding a democracy, this must not be forgotten, either in formulating rights for male and female citizens or in the way in which elections and political representation operate.

The foundations of democracy have, therefore, to be renewed as being-two, on the basis of a just relationship between two beings. *To Be Two* and *I Love To You* are trying to define this. This way of rethinking democracy is so right and fertile that, in trying to establish a code of citizenship on the European level, all I have done is meditate on how a political project, as, too, a civil relation between Renzo Imbeni and Luce Irigaray, could work: that is, between on the one hand an Italian male, ex-National Secretary of the FGCI, ex-mayor of Bologna and today a member of the European Parliament, in other words, a man who dedicates his life to

Democracy is Love

political activity in the framework of a party; and, on the other, a Frenchwoman, Director of Research in Philosophy with the CNRS, a leading figure in Women's Liberation both in her theoretical and practical activity, and who has no party allegiance.

The result has been positive, in the sense that the code of citizenship, envisaged in this way, was able to be shared by Renzo Imbeni and Luce Irigaray as European citizens; and insofar as it attracted a great deal of interest.

Of course, it has not yet been approved by the entire European Parliament. We'll have to be patient! Because nowadays political activity is all too often confused with economic power and even democracy with demagogy, in other words, with seducing the electorate rather than having its interests at heart.

Another reason for the delay in agreeing to, as, also, understanding, a project of this kind is the fact that, until the relationship between man and woman has changed, the desire to dominate nature, not only in the cosmos and women's nature but equally the nature of young people, of other races and of citizens of other countries and other cultures, will remain unchanged.

Only a new alliance and a new friendship between the genders, that is between nature and culture, will teach us how to develop other customs and other laws in respect for the other as other.

But we cannot simply wait and hope. We have to work at this task here and now, and change society not only by means of the decisions of political personalities, but democratically, starting with our own decisions: in the way we act, speak and exist.

I have set off along this path, in part with Renzo Imbeni, by writing my most recent books and in our shared work on citizenship of the European Union. I hope that all of you, women and men, will adopt a similar path towards greater justice and happiness both in ourselves and between us.

The Question of the Other

* Two uses of the term 'the other' should be distinguished throughout this chapter. The Italian 'l'altro' (masculine) appears without an asterisk; the more complex 'l'altro(a)', combining masculine and feminine, appears asterisked.

Western philosophy, perhaps all philosophies, have started from a singular subject. For centuries, no-one imagined that different subjects might exist and, more particularly, that man and woman might be different subjects.

Of course, from the late nineteenth century onwards, attention turned increasingly to the question of the other. The philosophical subject, by now more sociological in nature, became a little less imperialistic. The existence of identities different from his own was admitted: children, for example, or mad people, savages and workers.

Seminar held at the University of Verona at the invitation of 'Ariadne's Thread' and of the Department of Philosophy (30 April 1994).

Democracy Begins Between Two

Certain empirical differences were, then, to be respected; not everyone was the same and it was therefore important to be a little more attentive to others and to what made them different. Yet the fundamental model of the human being remained unchanged: one, singular, solitary and historically masculine, that of the adult Western male, rational, competent. Diversity was therefore still conceived of and lived hierarchically, with the many always subordinate to the one. Others were nothing but copies of the idea of man, a potentially perfect idea which all the more or less imperfect copies had to try to equal. These copies, moreover, were not defined in their own terms, in other words, according to a different subjectivity, but in those of an ideal subjectivity and as a function of their deficiencies with respect to it: age, race, culture, sex, etc. The model of the subject thus remained singular, and the 'others' represented more or less good examples within the hierarchy established in relation to the singular subject.

This philosophical model corresponds, in fact, to the political model of a single leader, judged the best, and the only one capable of governing more or less civil citizens possessed of a more or less human identity.

Such a conception of the other perhaps explains Simone de Beauvoir's refusal to be treated as an other*. Since she does not, as a woman, accept coming 'second' to the male subject, she claims subjective status as man's equal, as the same or similar to him.

On a philosophical level, this demand implies a

The Question of the Other

return to the singular subject, historically masculine, and the cancellation of the possibility of any subjectivity other than man's. Although Simone de Beauvoir's critical work on the devalorization of woman as culturally 'secondary' is often accurate, her refusal to consider the question of woman as 'other'* represents philosophically, and even politically, a significant regression. Her position is, in fact, retrograde as regards those of certain [male] philosophers who enquire into the possibility of relations between two or different subjects: existentialists, personalists or more political philosophers; and it is also less driven by that of women who are struggling for the recognition of an identity of their own.

Simone de Beauvoir's positive proposals contain, in my opinion, a theoretical and practical error inasmuch as they imply the negation of an other* of an equivalent value to that of the masculine subject.

THE OTHER: WOMAN

My work on female subjectivity develops in the opposite direction to that of Simone de Beauvoir's work as regards the question of the other*.

Instead of saying as she does: I do not wish to be the other* of the masculine subject and, in order to escape this secondary position, I claim to be equal to him, I argue: the question of who the other is has not been well formulated in the Western tradition, in which the other is always the other of a singular subject and not another subject, irreducible to the masculine subject and of equal dignity.

This means that in our tradition there has not yet really existed an other for the philosophical subject and, more generally, for the cultural and political subject.

> In the subtitle of *Speculum of the Other Woman*, – the other is to be understood above all as a noun. In French, but also in other languages such as Italian and English, this noun is usually read as designating both man and woman. In this subtitle, I wanted to indicate that, in reality, the other is not neutral, neither grammatically nor semantically, and that it is not, no longer, possible to use the same term, in an undifferentiated way, to refer to the masculine and the feminine. Now this is, in fact, what happens in philosophy, religion and politics. The existence of the other, love of the other, concern for the other, etc. are evoked, without the question of who or what this other represents being asked. The lack of definition of the alterity of the other has paralysed thought, the dialectical method included, in an idealistic dream appropriate to a single (masculine) subject, in the illusion of a singular absolute, leaving religion and politics to an empiricism fundamentally lacking in ethics insofar as respect between individuals is concerned. In fact, if the other is not defined in his actual reality, he remains another me, and not a real other. In this case, he can be *more* or *less* than I, he can have more or less than I have. The Other can

thus represent absolute greatness and perfection: God, Master, Logos; he can designate the smallest or the most vulnerable: children, sick people, poor people, strangers; he can name the one whom I believe equal to me. In all of this, there is not really any other, but rather only the same: smaller, greater, equal to me. (*I Love To You*, p. 61)

Rather than refusing, as Simone de Beauvoir does, to be the other gender, the other sex, I am asking to be recognized as really an other*, irreducible to the masculine subject. I can now see just how much the subtitle of *Speculum* may have irritated Simone de Beauvoir: *Of the other as woman*. At that time I sent her my book in good faith, hoping for her support with the difficulties that I was facing at that point. I never received an answer and it was only recently that I understood the reason for her silence. Probably I offended her without wishing to. I had read the Introduction to *The Second Sex* long before I wrote *Speculum*, and I didn't remember what the problematic of the other in her work was. Perhaps she didn't understand that, for me, it wasn't a question of admitting that my sex and gender should remain 'second', but of wanting the sexes and the genders to become two, without there being a first or a second.

I was pursuing, in my way, and unaware of their work, a goal which was closer to that of militant American neo-feminism, a feminism that promotes difference, one more closely related to the cultural revolution of 1968 than the egalitarian feminism of Simone de Beauvoir. Let us recall, briefly, what is at stake here: the exploitation and the alienation of women are located in the difference between the sexes and the genders, and have to be resolved in that difference, without trying to abolish it, which would amount to yet another reduction to the singular subject. In *Speculum* what I am interpreting and criticizing is precisely the fact that the philosophical subject, historically masculine, has reduced every other to a relation with himself – his nature, his universe, his complement, his projection, his inverse, his instrument ... – within his own world, his own horizon.

Whether it is a question of Freud's work or of the most important philosophical systems of our tradition, I try to reveal how the other always remains the other of the subject himself, and not a real other.

So the criticisms which I level at Freud all come back to the same interpretation: he views the sexuality and, more generally the identity, of the little girl, the adolescent girl and the woman solely in terms of the sexuality and identity of the little boy, the adolescent boy and the man.

According to Freud, for example, the auto-eroticism of the little girl lasts for as long as she confuses her own clitoris with a little penis, for as long as she imagines she has the same sex organ as the little boy. When she discovers through the mother, that the woman does not have the male sex organ, the little girl renounces her

The Question of the Other

own feminine identity and turns to the father, to the man, to obtain the penis through them. All her energy is from now on, according to Freud, engaged in acquiring the male sex organ. Even conceiving and giving birth to a child correspond, in his view, to a desire to appropriate the penis or the phallus and, for this reason, the birth of a male child is preferable to that of a baby girl. For Freud, no marriage can be happy, and no woman a good wife, without the birth of a male child.

Nowadays such a description would make some of the women here, and even some of the men, laugh. Yet a few years ago, not even twenty, any woman who pointed out the frightening machismo of our culture was laughted at, and excluded from teaching in the university. But things are not yet as clear as it may seem. Agreed, we are no longer completely in the Dark Ages but, if Freudian theory is macho, this is because it reproduces our sociocultural order. In a sense Freud did not invent machismo, he simply described it. His mistake — as, too, Simone de Beauvoir's — concerns how to overcome it. Neither she nor he recognize the other as other and, in different ways, both propose retaining the man as the subjective model whom woman should, so to speak, try to 'equal'. For Freud and Simone de Beauvoir, man and woman, by different strategies, should become alike. This ideal remains obedient to that of traditional philosophy which imposes a singular model of subjectivity, historically masculine.

This singular model can, at best, allow for an oscillation between the *one* and the *many*, but the one remains more or less obviously in charge of the hierarchy of the many: the singular is unique and/but ideal, Man. Concrete singularity is only a copy, an image.

Plato's vision of the world, his conception of truth, is in a way an inversion of the empirical reality of everyday. You believe that you are real, a singular truth but, in fact, you are only a more or less accurate copy of a perfect idea situated outside you.

Here again, before laughing too soon, we have to consider the continuing relevance of such a conception of the world. We are children of the flesh but also of the word, we are nature but also culture. Now, if we are children of culture, we are children of the idea, that is, more or less appropriate incarnations of an ideal model. Often, in order to draw closer to it, we mime, imitate, like children, what we perceive as an ideal. All these ways of saying and doing derive from a Platonic matrix, are the inheritance of a masculine idea of the truth. Even in the reversal which the privilege of the many over the one represents, a contemporary reversal in the name, amongst other things, of democracy, even in the privileging of the other over the subject, that of the *thou* with respect to the *I*, (I am thinking, for example, of some of Buber's writings and of a part of Levinas' work, where such privileging is more moral and theological, perhaps, than philosophical), we remain subjected to a blind model of the one and the many, of the one and the same, a model on which a singular subject imposes one sense rather than an other. Similarly, granting precedence to concrete singularity over

The Question of the Other

ideal singularity is inadequate in challenging the authority of a universal valid for all men and all women. In reality, no concrete singularity can designate an ideal valid for all men and all women, and to ensure the coexistence of subjects, particularly on the civil level, a minimum of universality is necessary.

If we are to get away from the omnipotent model of the one and the many, we have to move on to the *two*, a two which is not two times one itself, not even a bigger or a smaller one, but which would be made up of *two* which are really different. The paradigm of this two is to be found in sexual difference. Why here? Because it implies two subjects who should not be situated in either a hierarchical or a genealogical relationship, and that these two subjects have the duty of preserving the human species and of developing its culture, while respecting their differences.

My first theoretical gesture was thus *to free the two from the one*, the two from the many, the other from the same, and to do this in a horizontal way by suspending the authority of the One: of man, of the father, of the leader, of the one god, of the unique truth, etc. It was a question of releasing the other from the same, of refusing to be reduced to the other* of the same, to an other (male) or an other (female) of the one, not becoming him, or like him, but constituting myself as an autonomous and different subject.

Obviously this gesture challenges our entire theoretical and practical tradition, and particularly Platonism, but without such a gesture we cannot speak of women's liberation, nor of ethical behaviour with regard to the other, nor of democracy. Without such a gesture philosophy itself risks suffocating, defeated by, amongst other things, the use of techniques which, since the origin and in the construction of the logos itself, threaten and undermine man's subjectivity, a victory which will be that much easier and more rapid in that woman no longer ensures the pole of nature which resists masculine *techné*.

Only the existence of two subjects can lead the masculine subject back to his own being, and this would be possible if woman had access to hers.

For this reason, it was necessary to free the feminine subject from the world of man, and to acknowledge this scandal for philosophy: the subject is neither one nor singular, but is two.

THE MEDIATIONS NEEDED BY THE FEMININE SUBJECT

It was essential to ensure that this barely defined feminine subject, lacking contours and edges, with neither norms nor mediations, have some points of reference, some guarantees, in order to nourish her and to protect her own becoming. After the critical phase of my work – a critique addressed to a monosubjective, monosexual, patriarchal and phallocratic philosophy and culture, – I tried to define the characteristics of the

The Question of the Other

feminine subject, characteristics which are indispensable to her affirmation as such, to avoid falling back into a lack of differentiation or into subjection to a singular subject.

One of the crucial means of assisting the becoming of the feminine subject, and thus my own becoming, was to escape from a single genealogical power, to affirm: I am born of man *and* of woman, and genealogical authority belongs to man *and* to woman.

Female genealogies had to be disinterred from oblivion, not simply to eliminate the existence of the father, in a kind of reversal dear to the most recent philosophers, but to return to the reality of the *two*. But it is true that it takes time to rediscover and re-establish this two and it cannot be the work of one woman only.

Besides rediscovering and being reconciled with female genealogies, it was necessary to give woman, women, a language, images and representations which were appropriate to them: on a cultural, and also on a religious, level, since 'God' has always been an important accomplice of the philosophical subject. I began to carry out this work in *Speculum, This Sex Which Is Not One, Sexes and Genealogies, Thinking the Difference* and in *Je, Tu, Nous*. In these works, I discuss the characteristics of a world in the feminine, a world different from that of man as regards relationships with language, with the body (age, health, beauty and, obviously, maternity), and relationships with work, nature, culture. Two examples: I try to show how life unfolds differently for woman than for man, in that her physical becoming is marked by more crucial stages – puberty, loss of virginity, maternity, menopause, – stages requiring a more complex becoming than that of man. A further example: in the context of work, I maintain, with the support of evidence, that socio-economic justice cannot be limited to the application of the rule: equal work for equal pay. This rule is not, in fact, applied though it also implies respect for, and valorization of, women as regards the choice of means and ends in production, as of professional qualifications, relationships in the workplace, etc.

In these books I also initiated a discourse on the necessity of specific rights for women. As I have written, women's liberation cannot develop unless it goes beyond this stage, which is indispensable both for social recognition and individual growth, and for community relationships, between women and between women and men. My juridical proposals aroused interest and mistrust: interest on the part of women who are not specialists in jurisprudence who recognize the importance of rights for themselves, interest also on the part of feminists in certain countries who, for a long time, have been concerned with juridical mediation as a step towards the liberation of humanity, and particularly of women.

Two currents of women's thought oppose this perspective. Women in favour of equality generally fail to appreciate why positive rights for women are necessary.

The Question of the Other

They fight to obtain rights equal to those of men, they struggle against discrimination but they neglect the fact that some of the choices which women have to make are different from men's, and that such choices cannot remain individual or private but have to be protected by law. I'm thinking, for example, of the freedom of choice in work patterns, but also in matters of sexuality, or reproduction, concerning custody of the children in the case of divorce or separation and, more generally, in the framework of intercultural marriages where the diversity of customs often makes matters problematic.

In my opinion, the lack of positive rights appropriate to women prevents them moving from a state of nature to civil status. Most of them still remain nature-bodies, subjected to State, Church, father and husband, lacking the statute of civil persons responsible for themselves and for the community.

Even women more in tune with the culture and politics of difference deny the need for civil rights specific to women because they fear the law as an instrument ensuring submission to the State. On the contrary, civil rights for individuals represent a guarantee for male and female citizens, because they allow them to oppose the authority of the State. They maintain a tension between individuals and the State, and can ensure the passage from a society of a state-dominated kind to a civil society, whose democratic character would be preserved by individual rights for its members.

I hope that women will understand and pursue the

goal of individual rights, both because such rights are necessary to them to protect and affirm their own identity, and because they are better prepared, as feminine subjects, to be interested in rights relating to individuals and to relationships between them, rather than simply in those which make up the bulk of masculine civil codes: rights of possession, of property ownership, of having as regards goods. What needs to be done is to complete already existing civil codes, constitutions and the Universal Declaration of Human Rights by adding rights for women and rights devised by women's spirit [genio femminile], that is, beyond sexed specificity, rights for male and female citizens as individuals.

THE OTHER: MAN

The uniqueness of this feminine spirit brings me back, in the final part of this talk, to the question of the other. Now that she has become an autonomous subject, woman, too, is obliged to situate herself in relation to the other, and the specificity of her identity leads her to privilege far more than man does the dimension of alterity in the process of subjective becoming. According to tradition, woman is the custodian of love, and is obliged to love, and in spite of all the misfortunes of love, without being given any reason for such a task.

I will certainly not become an accomplice to this kind of obligation with regard to love, nor to that duty with

The Question of the Other

regard to hate which, it seems to me, is its complementary principle.

I prefer to pass on to you results obtained from research into how women speak, and to put forward an interpretation of the characteristics of a language in female mode (cf. *I Love To You*).

The language which pays most attention to the other is that of the little girl. She addresses the other – in my sample, the mother – asking for an agreement to do something together: 'Mamma, can I play with you?', 'Mamma, can I comb your hair?' In such statements, the little girl always respects the existence of two subjects, both of whom have the right to speak. In addition, what she proposes is an activity involving two subjects. The young girl could be a model for both, including the mother, who addresses her daughter with words like these: 'Tidy up before you watch TV', 'Bring me some milk on your way back from school'.

The mother gives her daughter instructions with no thought of a right to speech for both subjects, nor does she invite any shared activity, involving two subjects. Strangely, the mother speaks to her little boy in a different fashion, showing more respect for his identity: 'Do you want me to come and kiss you goodnight before you go to sleep?'. As for the little boy, he already speaks like a little leader: 'I want to play ball, I want a little car'. Somehow the mother communicates to the little boy the *thou* that her daughter has given her.

Why such a taste for dialogue on the part of the little girl? Perhaps because as a woman, born of woman, with the properties and qualities of a woman, including those associated with giving birth, the little girl finds herself, from birth, better placed to enter into a relationship involving two subjects. This would explain her games with dolls, to whom she addresses a nostalgia for dialogue often left unsatisfied by the mother.

But the little girl will lose this, her first, feminine, partner in dialogue, as a result of her entry into a culture in which the subject is always masculine – he, He, they – whether it is a question of linguistic gender in the narrow sense or of various metaphors which supposedly represent human identity and its becoming.

Despite this, neither the little girl nor the adolescent girl renounces the relationship with the other, which they almost always prefer to the relationship with the object. Thus, when they are asked to form a sentence containing the preposition *with*, or the adverb *together*, female adolescents and students, and most adult women, will answer with statements like the following: 'I'll go out with him tonight', 'We'll always live together'; male subjects, for their part, tend to say: 'I came by [Ital. *con*] motor bike', 'I wrote this sentence with my pen', 'We get on well together, my guitar and I'.

A difference of this sort between the statements of subjects of the female gender and those of the male gender is expressed in one way or another in most of the replies given to questions whose aim was to define the sexed characteristics of language (this research is

The Question of the Other

being carried out in various languages and cultures, in particular, the Romance and Anglo-Saxon ones).

Besides the alternation between the male choice of the subject-object relation and the female choice of the subject-subject relation, other characteristics can be noted. Women privilege the present or the future tenses, contiguity, the concrete context, relationships based in difference, being together, being-two; men, on the other hand, privilege the past tense, a metaphorical use of language, abstract transposition, relations between like and like by way of the object, relationships between the one and the many.

Women and men rely, then, on different subjective configurations and ways of speaking. These cannot be attributed solely to socio-historical determinations, nor to an alienation of the feminine which is to be overcome by making it equal to the masculine. Women's language does, of course, give signs of a degree of alienation and inertia, but it also demonstrates a richness of its own which has nothing to envy in men's language; and, particularly a taste for intersubjectivity which is definitely not to be abandoned in favour of the subject-object relation dear to men.

How could the feminine subject – and, first and foremost, myself – cultivate sharing with the other without becoming alienated? The gesture to be made here corresponds to the one already made at the time of *Speculum*: practising respect for the other as other. I live, we live, as women, a nostalgia for dialogue and relationship. But have we yet reached the point of recognizing the other as other, and of addressing him or her as such? Not really, not yet. The words of adolescent girls and of women do, indeed, reveal a tendency to favour the relationship with the other, but the desire for the *I – thou* relationship does not always care who *thou* is, nor what *thou* might desire.

Thus the female subject privileges the relation with the other gender, which the masculine subject does not do. This prioritizing of the masculine as partner in dialogue is proof, on the one hand, of cultural alienation and demonstrates, on the other, various characteristics of the feminine subject. Woman knows the other gender better: she engenders it within herself, she mothers it from birth, she nourishes it from her own body, she lives it inside herself in love. Her relationship to the transcendence of the other therefore constitutes itself differently with regard to man, for whom the other always remains outside the subject; and for whom transcendence of the other is marked by a mystery and an ambivalence associated with the problem of the origin, whether maternal or paternal. Woman's relation to man is linked to a carnal sharing, to an experience of the sensibility, to an immanence that is lived, even in the producing of children. The alterity of the other imposes itself on her because of the extraneity of his behaviour, and because of the resistance which he opposes to her own dreams and intentions. But she must constitute the transcendence of the other in a horizontal way, through a sharing of life which respects

The Question of the Other

absolutely the other as other, beyond any intuition, any sense perception, any experiencing and knowledge. Women's inclination to dialogue runs the risk of reducing the other to a modality of herself unless she constructs the transcendence of the other as such, his irreducibility to herself through fusion, contiguity, empathy, mimetism, etc.

In *To Be Two* and *I Love To You* I've tried to open a path towards such a construction of the transcendence of the other. I have shown how the operation of the negative, which typically intervenes with a dialectic movement between self and self in order to reach a more spiritually evolved and cultivated becoming, ought to operate between two subjects, to prevent the reduction of the *two* to the *one*, of the other to the same.

Of course, the negative still intervenes in the development of my own subjectivity, but to delineate the irreducibility of the other to myself, and not to reduce its exteriority to myself. The subject, by a gesture of this kind, renounces being one and singular; instead, it respects the two in the intersubjective relation.

A gesture of this sort must intervene above all in the relation between the genders because alterity there is real and enables a new articulation of the relationship between nature and culture, in a more truthful and ethical way. It would thus be possible to overcome the guilt on which our culture is founded, which Hegel uncovered in speaking of the rejection and death of Antigone (*Phenomenology of Spirit*, Chap.VI).

Democracy Begins Between Two

The historical accomplishment of this passage from the subject as one and singular to the existence of two subjects of equivalent value and dignity seems to me an appropriate task for women as regards both philosophy and politics. Women, as I have already mentioned, are better able to commit themselves to a relationship between two, to the relationship with the other. Their subjectivity allows them to open up again the horizon of the one, the similar, and even of the many, in order to present themselves as an other subject, and to impose a two which is not a 'second'. Accomplishing one's own liberation implies, moreover, the recognition of the other as other to avoid the closing of the circle around the singular subject.

Recognizing man as an other thus represents not only an ethical task appropriate to women, but also an indispensable step towards the acquisition of their autonomy. The necessary deployment of the negative to respect the alterity of the other allows them to leave a solely natural identity behind and to accede to a civil identity without denying their own nature, thanks to their faithfulness to a gender identity.

All relationships with the other now involve a negative: in language, of course – for example; 'I love to you' and not 'I love you' – but also in perceiving, in listening, in touching. In *To Be Two* I try to define a new way of approaching the other, emphasizing how we can caress each other without losing either the *I* or the *thou*.

*

The Question of the Other

Carrying out this revolution, which goes from affirming the self as other to recognizing man as other, is a gesture which will then permit all the various forms of alterity to be respected without authority or hierarchy, whether one is dealing with race, age, culture, religion, etc.

Substituting the *two* for the *one* in sexual difference corresponds, then, to a decisive philosophical and political gesture, one which renounces being *one or many* in favour of *being-two* as the necessary foundation of a new ontology, a new ethics and a new politics in which the other is recognized as other and not as the same: greater, smaller, at best equal to me.

A Two-Subject Culture

Equality of opportunity[4] seems the greatest gift that our states and our cultures can offer to women. No, you are not inferior to men, our leaders keep telling us. The evidence? You have the right to jobs that are equal to theirs in society. A few statistics quickly reveal that this proclaimed equality, though a formal right, is not applied. If it were applied, and applicable, women would unquestionably occupy 50 per cent and more of all the positions involving social decision-making and responsibility. We are a long way from this!

So let us leave 'equality of opportunity' to its status as slogan.

The pressure exerted by women's liberation movements, sometimes heeded because a degree of political attention has been accorded it, has not been able to do more than offer 'equality of opportunity' to women.

Talk given at the seminar 'European and French contributions to equality of opportunity for girls and boys', organized by the Ministry for National Education and Culture, by the Secretariat for the Rights of Women and by the European Commissions (Paris, 22 May 1992). This text, published in French in 1993, was translated by Carla Ricci and Luce Irigaray.

A Two-Subject Culture

If we are to avoid doing them an even greater injustice, we must now seriously ask ourselves what meaning the political horizon of 'equality of opportunity' can have.

Since this is a European seminar, I would like to point out some of the differences in the way in which this 'equality of opportunity' is interpreted in different European countries.

I shall give three examples drawn from Europe in both its original and its enlarged form.

1. A legislative project concerning maternity leave in Sweden: six months for women and six months for men, *salvo deroga legale*. This measure could be called: how to make equal opportunities between the genders possible without making motherhood an obstacle to the right to work. The measure was proposed in the autumn of 1990. Statistics indicate that 45 per cent of men supported it. Despite this, the law was not passed in these terms. However, the legal possibility for men to share maternity leave, for shorter periods of time, remains.

2. Interest in working hours, for example part-time, in community creches and in shop-opening hours in Italy. These kinds of concern could be read as measures which make 'parity' of opportunity concerning the right to work possible for women and men. In Italy, it is worth noting, the expression 'parity of opportunity' is used. This seems to me more appropriate insofar as it suggests that opportunities should be equivalent for the two genders which does not necessarily mean equal.

Democracy Begins Between Two

3. The right for women to hold certain jobs, traditionally reserved for men, which was highlighted in a recent publicity campaign conducted by the French government to encourage the employment of young women in the technical sphere.

I'd like to underline certain points concerning the arguments used here:

– The terms in which this campaign was conducted are questionable. 'It's technical, it's for her' ('C'est technique, c'est pour elle'). This slogan was often accompanied by a smiling young woman. In fact, it has nothing to do with 'equality' of opportunity which would have to be formulated as: 'It's technical, it's for her *as well*'. Instead, it identifies technical work as a specifically female vocation. This opening-up of job opportunities adopts, in other words, a demagogical tone, rather than evoking a right to work that is identical for women and for men.

– The jobs in question generally require low qualifications. A counter-example; 'It's a decision-making job, it's for her'. Between being part of the technical executive or part of the decision-making process, in particular as regards the strategic choices made by the firm, there are obvious inequalities.

– The work that girls are offered – and dignity of labour does not even come into it – is not the best remunerated.

This campaign belongs within the framework of a new form of collusion between enterprise and edu-

A Two-Subject Culture

cation: 'It is pointless setting enterprise and education up as opponents. They complement each other, and the isolation of these two worlds with their mutual distrust of each other's intentions has for too long been damaging to the interests of both individual citizens and to society as a whole' (cf. 'Trump', letter from ONISEP to secondary school teachers, March 1992).

And it is girls who are to test out this new 'alliance' (?) between economy and culture. The educational opportunities recently made available to them can therefore be reduced to the economic imperative. That is what unemployment dictates!

The 'equality' of opportunity offered by this campaign appears, then, as an invitation to girls, who are not equipped to decipher the real motive behind the proposal, to adapt themselves to the society of men and to lend it their assistance wherever it has need.

'It's technical, it's for her' does not strike me as all that different, despite appearances, from the 'return to the home' which Frenchwomen were offered a few years ago. Is housework not 'technical' as well, in a certain sense? And does this technical recruitment not amount to an invitation to women to return to the home, in other words, to occupations which they have always been involved in and which deprive them of the hope of a better cultural training and thus of a better qualified job?

In this context, nothing has been done about finding out what women's specific requirements and desires might be, particularly as far as work is concerned. The decision has been taken based on economic imperatives that have nothing to do with them: the requirements of the firm which they must obey (yet again!) and whose development, it seems a foregone conclusion, they will have no power to modify.

I could give other examples. But these are sufficient, I think, to demonstrate that the perspective of 'equality of opportunity' can be interpreted as follows: being concerned with women's problems in order to help them enter the social world, particularly the job market, or opening up a little side-door to allow women into male society on condition that they prove themselves up to it.

By pointing out various interpretations of proposals concerning 'equality of opportunity' which relate to the right to work, I have perhaps still not identified the nub of the problem. I have indicated some of the measures, more or less concerned with women, which the 'equality of opportunity' objective between men and women involves. These measures are often prompted by concern for the family and not therefore for women as such.

It is worth bearing this in mind and not forgetting it. Allowing women the choice to get married, to have children *and* to work is not a recognition of them as women.

*

A Two-Subject Culture

On this subject I would like to put forward some suggestions and observations.

Entering the world of work as it is defined by men does not yet mean having the right to work as women. The right to work should imply, for example, being able to choose one's working objectives and conditions and, amongst these, one's working hours.

Now, 'equality of opportunity' is very little concerned with such problems, as far as I can judge. If women have, in some countries, taken the initiative with so-called alternative types of work and production, this has, I think, been as a result of a personal decision, with the risks that this entails, rather than with the help of existing institutions.

'Equality of opportunity' ought to imply creating objectives and conditions of work suitable for women. If not, 'equality of opportunity' does not exist. At best what we have seen is tolerance of a certain number of women entering the world of production as it is defined by men. This is not 'equality' of opportunity.

'Equality of opportunity' therefore means opening up new sectors in the world of work, sectors which are appropriate to women, both on the level of their tastes or ethical choices and on that of their possibilities: physical, familial, etc. So I am a little doubtful as to whether women enjoy manufacturing arms. I believe that they would prefer to contribute to the existence of a society where intersubjective relations are more enjoyable, in other words, to create jobs, environments, meeting places, for example. Interior decorating, looking after city parks, working to improve public relations etc. should meet with their approval.

Women also like social work: work which brings people together, involving a bond between citizens, male and female, or helping the community. They have a gift for this kind of work, and they do it with competence and enjoyment.

Strangely these social sectors, where women are by far in the majority, are underpaid, require no training, lack any technological equipment, and are undervalued by our culture, which nonetheless finds time to be concerned about poverty in distant lands.

Although politicians still lend an ear to factory workers, I rarely hear them talking about the female social workers who provide meals or are cleaners in schools, or who look after sick people in their homes. And all of this for a pittance, more often than not, and above all without any recognition on the part of society.

More generally, all the occupations involving nurses, social assistants in the narrow or wider sense, teachers or support workers for social services or in public relations, occupations in which women are clearly in the majority, are simultaneously underpaid and without value or even visibility in terms of civil society.

'Equality of opportunity' would mean revalorizing these more female professions, revalorizing them economically and culturally.

This is not the path that we have chosen to follow: the old village schoolmistress was, as far as I can judge,

A Two-Subject Culture

much more highly prized as a personality in the past than she is nowadays.

We have constant proof of this devalorizing of the female professions: nurses' strikes, the downgrading of the teaching profession, placing teaching in second place to economic production.

Nor are professional qualifications stated in terms appropriate to female identity. Yet the designation of the professional level is important. And, as part of the desire to pay women salaries equal to men's, it is essential to valorize their work in a way that is appropriate to female identity. Without this, it is impossible to speak of an 'equality' of opportunity.

If, in order to be director [Ital. *direttrice* gram. fem.] of research at the CNRS (the French CNR), I have to call myself director [Ital. *direttore* gram. masc.] of research, I am not enjoying 'equality of opportunity'. All I have is the possibility of inserting myself more or less furtively and easily into the opportunities offered to men. And that is a very different thing! It is not equitable that my work is not be recognized, from the economic and cultural viewpoint, in terms of my identity as a woman.

The rest is just a question of power, whatever the learned arguments put forward to justify it.

Arguments like these concerning the so-called neutralization of gender at the professional level, are sometimes supported by feminists who look on belonging to a gender as nothing but a form of oppression. If being woman has meant, and still means, for women, being exploited, being woman also means belonging to half the world's population; and having the right to have one's own identity recognized seems to me to be part of equality of opportunity, for both genders.

How are we to define the difference between woma(e)n and ma(e)n? How can it be made clear that they are two, irreducible the one to the other?

Denouncing the oppression of one by the other is not enough. Abolishing the reality of the genders to resolve the domination of one by the other does not make much sense, and brings danger for humanity itself in its wake.

Gender alienation occurs as a result of the reduction of the two to the one: the human gender, so-called universal and neutral.

This alienation cannot be overcome by abolishing what remains of the 'two', but rather by affirming the differences between woma(e)n and ma(e)n and granting equivalent values to the two genders.

What does the difference between woma(e)n and ma(e)n consist of? The error has been to want to quantify or enumerate a difference which is of another nature than one which can be described, evaluated, counted.

If I consider some of the differences between woma(e)n and ma(e)n, differences which form part of their subjectivity and are not related to variations which

A Two-Subject Culture

reduce one and the other (male and female) to objects of scientific scrutiny (sociology, psychology, biology, etc.) which have no interiority of their own, I cannot avoid the conclusion that woma(e)n and ma(e)n represent two different worlds, two visions of the world which remain irreducibly distinct.

Thus the following factors determine a different structuring of subjectivity:

– being born of the same gender or of a different gender from one's own: being the daughter of a mother or the son of a mother;

– whether or not one can conceive a living being in one's own body;

– whether one procreates within oneself or outside oneself;

– whether one can nourish another living being from one's own body or only through one's own labour.

Events of this kind, which are differently organized in the life of a woman or of a man, create two identities, two ways of looking at the world, which cannot be reduced to one.

Ma(e)n and woma(e)n are other, genuinely distinct. Every reduction of their difference(s) to equality brings with it a reduction of their specific subjectivities and of the possibility of fruitful, living relationships between them.

In addition to the economic exploitation described by Marx, there exists another, less analysed, form of exploitation: that of the subjectivity and of the identity of one of the two human genders by a given culture, a given

Democracy Begins Between Two

society. We have not yet gone as far as we could in interpreting this kind of exploitation, nor in researching possible remedies.

Woma(e)n and ma(e)n are therefore different, more different than Black and White, Catholic and Moslem, European and Oriental. They are different in the constitution of their subjectivity, and in their way of looking at the world.

In order to try to highlight, understand and take these differences into account I conducted – with the help of international research teams, as can be seen, for example, in *Sexes and Genealogies* – enquiries into the ways in which women and men speak, their ways of living love, culture, relationships involving the civil and religious representation of their gender, the other gender and of the community.

I will now list some of the traits specific to women and men which have been identified on the basis of their responses to these enquiries.

Women generally privilege:

– intersubjectivity;

– the relationship with the other gender (for good and bad reasons: the choice of the masculine comes about as the result of language and culture and is not really a free one);

– the physical environment, including the natural one;

– the present or future tense.

Men, on the contrary, generally choose:

A Two-Subject Culture

– the subject-object relation;
– the construction of a work or a world rather than respecting what already exists independently of them, in other words, creating a world of their own without regard for the already existing reality;
– the use of instruments: the hand, the tool in the narrow sense, language, all forms of mediation and mediators;
– relationships between the one and a plurality which remains loosely defined: people, others, the nation;
– the representation of the world as made up of abstract, inanimate entities: notions (social justice, human species), ideas (the truth), events (the Treaty of Maastricht), ideals or life horizons (equality of opportunity);
– the past determining the present and the future.

For a clarification of the method of enquiry and an analysis of the results, I refer you to *I Love To You, The Time of Difference, Je, Tu, Nous*.

The education offered to pupils of both sexes appears, therefore, to be of a type which is defined on the basis of a masculine culture, perhaps suitable for educating boys but not necessarily girls. This fact can be easily explained from an historical point of view: it is not all that long since girls started attending school.

Teaching of this sort favours:
– the training of the subject by means of knowledge,

Democracy Begins Between Two

a knowledge that is to be acquired, and not a process of becoming subject in the context of relations with other subjects;

– the rule of the subject over the world rather than respect for and understanding of life and the existing universe;

– the acquisition of instruments, knowledges, of skills, rather than of rules of civilization, in particular for life in the community;

– each subject entering a world of one + one + one largely indeterminate individuals, unless it is in terms of their competence, in particular as regards the use of a technique and the fabrication of objects;

– submission to a tradition rather than concern for the present and constructing a livable and more cultured future;

– acquiring ideas and abstract notions with no regard for the physical environment, etc.

In our educational system, the feminine way of looking at the world is thus seen from the outset as subordinate to the masculine way.

Giving girls and boys an 'equality' of opportunity means nowadays that feminine identity has to be explored, questions have to be asked about the individual and social qualities of such an identity, and the means of elaborating a culture based on it have to be developed.

Girls, women, outside the family home, have, or at least should have, become citizens in the full sense of

A Two-Subject Culture

the term. Granting them equality of opportunity cannot be restricted to allowing them to enter a world geared to men's qualities and needs, but must involve finding out what their specific qualities are in order to review their education and their professional life in the light of these qualities.

A change of perspective of this sort leads to respecting women as mature citizens, and to the enrichment of the community with values which it needs: the practice of intersubjectivity, the sense of the concrete, concern for the future; and to enabling coexistence between women and men, not only on the instinctual level – with all the forms of violence which the institution of the family modestly conceals – but on the level of civilization.

Equality or parity of opportunity between the genders requires us to open up a new horizon for the civil community and for human culture.

But it is better to have possibilities for the future than to be already totally determined by the past.

And it is better, too, to remain living persons: men and women, than to become neutral, abstract, artificial individuals, members of a social machine which functions more or less efficiently, but with no possibility of being governed, and in which identity and relationships between persons come second to the rule of money and to the arbitrary authority of certain decisions.

Ten Suggestions for the Construction of the European Union

1) We live in a society dominated by needs, dominated by the relationship to money. In this context, how are we to set up a form of citizenship at the European level which takes individuals and the relationships between them into account?

We talk of being interdependent and of how we must all share. But not everyone thinks like this, not everyone is ready to share. So what is to be done? What is more, an obligation of this kind, although fair in a sense, still belongs within a paternalistic model: the richest have to help the poorest. This form of sharing makes up, I fear, for past errors but in no way looks forward to a different future.

It would appear, then, that we have to find a new way of articulating the dialectic of relationships between individuals and of relationships between goods. It often strikes me that the various fascisms, racisms, holocausts

---

Suggestions sent to Renzo Imbeni for the European Electoral Campaign (7 May 1994).

Ten Suggestions for the Construction of the EU

etc. are, in fact, the product of more or less conscious economic motives. Calling on the generosity of individuals is thus not enough if we are to escape dangers of this sort. The question is more complex and, as I have already stated, implies a modification of the relations between individuals and goods. In this respect, too much time is spent, in my view, on condemning and judging and too little on thinking, planning ahead and making changes.

2) In the context of work and of having a job, what seems to be particularly lacking is any consideration of the respect felt by individuals with regard to the production of goods so that these become, in a sense, their masters instead of being at their service. This should be cause for reflection.

As regards unemployment nowadays, for example, remarks like the following can be heard: you should increase consumption if you want to create jobs; the State has to inject money to create more work; more and more new and equally useless products have to go on being invented if we're to absorb unemployment, etc. Solutions of this sort presuppose a society based not on individuals but on money which, in effect, makes a civil community impossible. In addition, conceiving of work in this way strips workers of human dignity.

In this respect, I am pretty much in accord with Jacques Delors' proposals which suggest creating jobs to protect the environment, for example, in the fight against pollution. As he rightly says: there has been too much exploitation of natural resources in recent years and too little human labour. This tendency has to be reversed by creating employment which serves natural resources.

Thinking about job creation in this fashion seems a fairer way of respecting human dignity and the dignity of work. Furthermore, jobs of this sort lend themselves more easily to community sharing than does the production of goods which plays on competition between citizens, cities, regions and nations.

3) Already at the national level, proposing the protection of the environment as a political task seems a way of ensuring both individual survival and coexistence in the community. The environment is, after all, a shared inheritance and looking after it ought to draw citizens, male and female, together without competitiveness or conflict. Moreover, taking responsibility for the environment goes along with respect for both the life of the individual and of the community. This, too, should, today, figure in political programmes.

The importance of these points is even more relevant at the European level since it is a question of ensuring a communal framework through respect for individual features in a way that should avoid provoking conflict and nationalism. In addition, in a supranational community, it is important for everyone, male and female, that each person — at every level: national, regional, individual – should take responsibility both for health and for the environment in which we live.

4) Often the help which we plan to give to less wealthy countries is a way of imposing industrialization as we know it on them. This strikes me as highly ambiguous. We know what the relationship between industrialization, capitalism and human slavery is. We also know what the limits of industrialization are as regards employment, yet we go on involving other countries in this process and, in this way, win a few more years for an economic regime whose blind alleys should be all too obvious to us.

In my view, it would be fairer politically-speaking to encourage a form of economic development that was appropriate to the environment and culture of a country, in other words to promote economic diversity rather than imposing a single and inevitably competitive model.

5) In addition to the dictatorship of money, the dignity of the human person and coexistence encounter a further danger nowadays in the power of technology and of the media. Male and female citizens are thus, at every instant, threatened with a loss of human identity. Little by little, no longer regulated by the relation to the self and to others, they become a neutral, abstract form of energy. As 'robots' they can still produce and consume, endlessly even, but they have lost sight of

what a culture of life and of coexistence means. In this sort of context, the worst scenario is possible; and does, indeed, already feature in political programmes either in the form of proposals that are solely economic or as a result of what such programmes conceal or elide.

6) In this respect, we have to reconsider the separation of the civil and the religious dimensions. Our lives are still governed by an implicit concordat according to which civil politics takes care of goods and the Church of individuals. This implies, for example, that the topic of the family is viewed as the responsibility of the Church, or at the most of the Christian Right, and not an appropriate responsibility for the Left.

This is why some women in the PDS explained to me that they had abandoned discussion of the family to the Right some years ago and, on the other hand, why people sometimes claim that I must be on the right since I'm trying to define a new relation for the couple and am not afraid of speaking about the need to transform coexistence in the family.

Now the basis of a civil community is not solely or primarily separate individuals, but individuals who are linked together by bonds, particularly of a sexed or family nature.

7) Remaining for a moment with the problem of the family, I would add that leaving the family unchanged is a way of allowing economic power to grow by preserving an aspect of life in a state of relative 'secur-

Ten Suggestions for the Construction of the EU

ity'. The production and consumption of goods serves, the argument goes, to build the family nest. But fantasizing and arguing along these lines does not stand up to the facts.

One only has to reveal the lack of coexistence at a civil, or simply human, level permeating the family, to see that it has to be rebuilt in terms of civil respect between its members: between man and woman, parents and children. Nowadays this need to renew the foundations of the family is even more urgent because of the mingling of cultures which implies coexistence and conflict between different traditions, norms and rules for living.

I believe that protecting family coexistence by means of civil rights between both men and women and parents and children is anyhow inevitable. This obligation could, moreover, be a way of moving towards a greater measure of happiness in the family, by transcending the immediacy of instinct and emotion in the direction of more human, less animal, relationships, which would not fit quite so easily into a model of domination and possession of the master-slave variety.

Of course, changing the way of relating within the framework of the family represents the point or site of major resistance. But why should this site remain blind, closed? Who stands to gain by this?

8) So we cannot run away from the problem of rethinking our civil codes, our constitutions and charters of human rights. Strangely, proposals of this sort

come up against distrust or outright rejection in certain quarters. Perhaps it's because I'm a Frenchwoman that I take rights in favour of the individual to mean rights allowing him/her a means of legal opposition to the State.

Rights for the individual do not mean increased subjection to the State but, on the contrary, a protection against state, national or supranational power. They make possible a positive historical tension between the State and each citizen, male and female. The failure to provide juridical protection for the rights of each person, male and female, leaves much more space for arbitrary, authoritarian power, which operates without the mediation which the law offers. Certain changes, for example, concerning parliamentary majority threaten to deprive women – but not only women – of gains that are not protected by law.

Of course, one can object here that a parliamentary majority can change the law. And this is true. We have not yet reached 'paradise'; we are still part of the process of History in the making. But it is harder to change the law – especially if there is a balance between national and supranational – than to do away with advantages which have no juridical protection.

9) Redefining rights for individuals is, moreover, an indispensable task at the level of the constitution of an enlarged community like Europe. The construction of the European Union cannot be carried out solely at the

Ten Suggestions for the Construction of the EU

economic level, without running the risk of an increasing loss of identity and, I believe, of vitality for each man and woman. We have to think of a new form of citizenship which takes account both of a wider community and of the fact that such a community now embraces people of varying cultures, races and traditions.

Even with regard to citizens' rights, codes vary from country to country and a certain unification of rights across the European Community cannot be avoided. To have the possibility of referring to a written text is essential as a form of democratic mediation to which every citizen, male and female, can refer and appeal.

10) In our times, the way in which we live often represents a danger to human life and consciousness. As well as being subjected to pollution, we are in the hands of a technical world which controls us. We are under increasing levels of stress, forced to work, and quite simply to live, at an ever faster rate which leaves no time to think, to remember, to create a human history. So it is essential to preserve an attentiveness to human culture, to its past and its future, as a way of protecting human life, consciousness and civilization.

Culture must not become a space for producing and consuming just like others, as the tendency often now is, but a place for remembering and creating human identity and coexistence. We should not, for example, simply find out all about other cultures, but ask our-

Democracy Begins Between Two

selves how we are to go beyond this abundance of information. How to set off in a direction that is neither cultural capitalism nor infinite dispersal but, rather, a further step historically in the accomplishment of human becoming?

Politics and Happiness

Clelia Mori made me very happy when she asked me to come and talk to you about politics and happiness. This topic is similar to the subtitle of *I Love to You: Sketch for a Felicity in History*.

Indeed happiness, whether private or public, personal or collective, is the goal which I have been pursuing for some years.

Of course, you can object that the world is sick, that talk of happiness is inappropriate; and some may even retort that happiness is not to be found on earth, though perhaps in heaven.

I believe that limiting oneself to this sort of argument results in an ever greater and more serious state of sickness. If happiness is for the afterlife, then there is no need to work towards its coming here below. And if all we can talk about is how sick the world is, then we are a long way from building another one: the kind of world that we want, that we desire.

Talk given during the European Electoral Campaign, at the invitation of Clelia Mori and the Federation of the PDS (Reggio Emilia, 6 June 1994).

Democracy Begins Between Two

So we remain in a state of permanent despair as regards our present and future life, we remain powerless, unable to make plans. We complain, we are critical, but we do not build a better world for today and for tomorrow.

This dearth of projects and positive initiatives is no good either to each of us, male and female, or to the community. Rather, it destroys us, first of all spiritually and then physically; what is more, it undoes social bonds. Each of us, male and female, as, too, our human collectivities, needs hope and energy which will create bridges between today and tomorrow, between the I and the others. Criticizing, despairing, hating do not create bonds but instead exploit energies that destroy them. Projects, hope, love, on the contrary, make bonds within and between us possible.

Why have we reached the point of being unable to plan, to love, to hope? Perhaps because we now find ourselves, male and female, exiled from ourselves, swamped by manufactured products which are too big and too numerous, too foreign to us, too distant from us. We are lost, not in a natural wood, which would cause us to feel anguish but would not exile us from ourselves, particularly from our sensibility. We would still be able to listen to the birds, to look at the trees and the flowers, to perceive the light and the heat of the sun and to find our way thanks to it. Being immersed in a concrete city is a totally different thing; we are now lost in another way, more dependent now,

Politics and Happiness

more the victims of the universe which controls us, transformed into 'yes-men' who have forgotten their own direction unless the manmade environment points it out to them.

As Sartre notes, the can-opener, the passage in the underground, street signs, T.V. programmes are what now dictate my path. They tell me what I have to do with no regard for my freedom, my initiative. Nowadays, we claim the right to our freedom all the more because we are imprisoned in a world of can-openers, underground passages, street signs and T.V. programmes. We appeal to the other, to others, for our freedom without understanding that changing the world which imprisons us is the first thing to be done.

We have seen that capitalism treats differently the one who possesses and the one who works, but we have not perceived clearly enough that its products alienate all of us, male and female, turning each and everyone of us into interchangeable numbers in a dehumanized world.

How then can we unite politics and happiness?

In my view, by refusing to accept that politics should be reduced to managing a world that is now dehumanized and dehumanizing; by refusing to accept that the world should remain as it is, criticizing only other people, as bad, within such a world. Nor is it enough to turn our attention to the distant horizon, to those worse off than ourselves, while continuing to obey the dictates of this world. All this leads to very little except accelerating the destruction of the human species and of its culture. And we should not delude ourselves that History can redeem all our mistakes. This sort of dreaming is no longer valid: humanity, particularly industrial capitalism, has put the planet itself in danger and there will not be a future unless we make the salvation of the earth itself our immediate concern.

Such an objective seems to me, today, to be the first one that we should pursue to ensure for each man and woman at least the right to life: to air, to water, to light, to the heat of the sun, to the nourishment of the earth. Rescuing the planet Earth means, too, being concerned about happiness, as much for ourselves as for others. Happiness of this kind does not cost much, has nothing to do with economic calculations – or, at least, it should not have – but is, perhaps, the highest form of happiness if we learn how to perceive it, to contemplate and to praise it.

What brings greater happiness than the return of spring? What is more marvellous than the lengthening of the days, than the earth once more covering itself in leaves and flowers and fruits? What is more joyful than the birds beginning to sing again? All this happiness which we receive for nothing should be given priority protection by a politics which is concerned with the well-being of each and everyone of us. It is a simple happiness, a universal happiness, a happiness which does not involve competitiveness or aggression, but, on the contrary, favours a rational and sensible sharing at both the national and supranational levels.

Politics and Happiness

When a politician like Jacques Delors argues that we should now be creating jobs which serve nature, for example in the fight against pollution, rather than ones which lead to yet further exploitation of natural resources, my faith in politics is slightly restored. Perhaps some politicians are beginning to understand that they have to deserve the trust of those, male and female, who elect them: first and foremost, by respecting their lives, the possibility of happiness which each person has, without colluding in the perversion of humanity's taste through technical products which are largely useless and through promises of an illusory well-being based on the possession of goods.

In fact, the ownership of goods does not make us happier. Of course, we need to eat, to dress ourselves, to have a home, but owning a lot of furniture, a lot of clothes, a lot of money does not represent the path to happiness. Sometimes, quite the reverse, this kind of ownership distances us from the joy of being in nature or with others. Our possessions create a screen between nature and ourselves, between others and ourselves.

We are afraid of losing what we already possess, we are always wanting more, we envy those who possess more than us and we start competing with them. Our attention, our intentions, our time are dedicated to the acquisition and preservation of possessions. We are no longer in any sense available towards ourselves, no longer able to find ourselves again in nature or with others.

Democracy Begins Between Two

These two forms of happiness have become obscured by things that encumber us, divide us and tear us apart within ourselves and between us. So we lose the possibility of coming back to ourselves as subjectively singular, as singular in our sensibilities, which would safeguard us from being submerged in an abstract and anonymous crowd, from being reduced to a 'yes-man', simply part of a common energy whose diverse potential has been neutralized.

We forget our human being and its principal resources: one's own becoming, our shared becoming. And this permits the emergence of an authoritarian leader or of a technology which destroys bodies, feelings, thought.

The sites of resistance to such dangers are the same as those which can bring us happiness: sharing with nature, exchange with others.

To establish or rediscover this sort of exchange with others, starting again from being-two, seems to me to provide a way that is both realistic and democratic. Realistic because, if I take my starting point in the crowd and its leader, I can never get back to being-two; the one and the many will have cancelled the two and the crowd will have destroyed singularity without respecting it.

Politicians (particularly those on the Left?) have not given enough thought to how to build a community without eliminating the singularity of each individual. Perhaps because, historically male, they were more

Politics and Happiness

concerned with relationships with the object, whether material or spiritual, than with relationships between subjects. Perhaps also because they imagined that they could bring a crowd together on the sole basis of needs, forgetting about subjective desires and aspirations. But, in fact, this cannot be done. I would also point out that they left responsibility for subjective relations to the domestic hearth and, in another sense, to the religious community, which did not favour a culture of coexistence between citizens. These politicians forgot, moreover, that the civil community is composed of men and women, and that ignoring this reality already constitutes an injustice as well as being an idealistic projection of society.

Beginning again from two, two that are different, man and woman, represents a way of overcoming this historical impasse as regards the formation of groups, of parties, of civil communities. In order to refound society on a democratic basis, we have to start again from the dialogue in difference, from a two which would not only be a couple in the intimacy of the domestic hearth, but a couple in a civil, political sense.

The human being has always, in our tradition, been thought of as one, singular, encompassing various modalities but always according to a hierarchy, for example, children, savages, workers, women, etc. Thus, being expresses itself through the one and the many, but the one always remains the model for the many. In our times, many men and women have overthrown the merit of the one in favour of the many: for them, only the plural can have truth value. This is the form that the social ideal of democracy must adopt.

Now, the plural thought of in this way, as well as being inadequate for ensuring social bonds, remains tied to the one and involves the power of the one insofar as it forms part of the same model.

I have been searching for a possible way of safeguarding being, without, for all that, contributing to the power of the one. I have therefore promoted 'being-two'.

In this being-two, being I is always regulated by another being: one is masculine, the other feminine. This new model allows us to translate the recent struggles for women's emancipation and liberation into words that can be shared, into private and public representations without separatism between the genders. This happier, more fertile and democratic model enables us, moreover, to turn to the many without hierarchizing, thanks to the respect of the difference between the one (male and female) and the other (male and female). From now on I can look at and encounter the other (male and female) – whether s/he is of another race, age, culture, religion, etc. – without feeling myself the superior one, nor the one who is simply a part of a whole whose governance can be appropriated by any leader whatever.

'Being-two', if it represents a more realistic, just and happy way of initiating coexistence in the community, also opens up a way for both men and women to return to the self, and thus to be able to resist the power of techniques, of abstract universalism, of the reduction of the world to one vast competitive market, all things which bring in their wake powerlessness and despair.

In my view, it is not possible to rediscover this path back to the self in any other way that brings both vitality and happiness. Anything else falls back into the opposition of the one and the many, into subjection to the power of money and the media, which leads progressively to the annihilation of the human being.

'Being-two', in addition to being between two, man and woman, thus invents a new way of being together for the community, for society. It is a question, first of all, of transforming the way that we relate between us, every moment of the day, and of doing so now in a more concrete and real fashion, more fruitfully and with greater happiness. To encourage and protect such a change, the fundamental institutional mediation should primarily be that of appropriate civil rights for all persons.

I hope that a programme of this sort, which is both simple yet feasible by all, women and men, will stimulate the interest of women, of young people and of men who are still concerned about life and happiness, for themselves, for each and every one of us.

The Representation of Women

Recently we have seen – and it is not the first time – the collapse of a certain idea of democracy: it is enough to be elected with a majority to be democratic. I say 'It is not the first time' because it is easy to remember that Hitler was democratically elected with a majority. So the question is not so simple.

Perhaps the only way of pursuing the democratic path nowadays is to achieve its objective, that is, to give citizens not only a right to vote but to give each man and each woman full political rights and duties. We have to entrust each man and each woman with an individual, if I can put it this way, political responsibility, and not entrust it to some leader, male or female.

Realizing democracy fully in this way means transferring a large part of the power of state bodies to the responsible autonomy of civil society. Some will object that we need the mediation of civil institutions. But the reply is fairly simple: institutional mediation is, in that

---

Speech made on the occasion of the European Electoral Campaign, at the invitation of Anna Maria Latina and of the Federation of the PDS (Pesaro, 8 June 1994).

The Representation of Women

case, a civil code of the rights and duties of each man and each woman towards the self and towards the community.

I am well prepared to make such a proposal for three reasons perhaps. The first is that I am a woman, a woman who favours women's liberation; and that we won the first new rights obtained for women, for each woman, without the opinion of lawyers or, initially, of Parliament. This seems to me to be one of the democratic moves that have been accomplished in recent years. I'll give two further examples. Working class struggles did not wait for legal judgment, nor even that of state representation, in demanding changes to rights, for example, in the sphere of work. The third example: French citizens, men and women, at the time of the so-called French Revolution, did not turn to the competent jurisprudence nor to already existing state bodies in order to impose a new civil code.

These three examples of the winning of specific civil rights on the part of male and female citizens seem to me to have been somewhat overlooked! Nowadays, in my view, male and female citizens place too much responsibility on self-styled experts – juridical or political – in the management of their own rights and duties. Perhaps we have become too old, too subservient to the power of the specialists, too enfeebled, to be conscious of our rights and to fight for our civil responsibilities.

Now, there are three reasons why we should return to civil responsibility.

Democracy Begins Between Two

The first is the one that is troubling you so much right now: what will become of the rights of Italian citizens, and particularly female citizens, as a result of the present government?

The second reason which, in my view, is not troubling you enough is: how are we to create a European citizenship, to attain a supranational, multicultural and multiracial citizenship, without it being to the detriment of the rights of each of the individuals who will make up the European Union? In other words, the problems posed by the European Union oblige us to go back and and bring about a real democracy. But we have to be careful to give these problems an adequate response: that is, as I see it, to reinforce the rights of each citizen, male and female, in order to entrust him or her both with respect for his/her own uniqueness and with the duty to respect the differences.

The third reason has to do with women's liberation. What meaning does being a woman have nowadays if this being, which is of a natural origin, is not guaranteed by a civil identity? What does it mean, for a woman, to be considered as a worker or a mother without any objective mediation guaranteeing her identity as a woman, either for herself or with regard to other women and men? And, again, what does it mean, for a woman, to represent other women without the mediation of civil rights? What are we to call a relationship of this kind? Power in masculine mode? Authority in feminine mode? What is this new way for women to relate amongst themselves all about? About a form of

The Representation of Women

reproduction, in the social and political sphere, of a familial model? Or about what then?

I believe that all these points have to be thought and defined juridically if they are to call themselves new forms of democracy. For me, a democratic relationship between a female representative and those, female, represented, is not possible unless there is a written text guaranteeing the rights of both parties. The woman represented has to be able to make reference to a written code if she is to be able to discuss her rights and responsibilities. For years, this sort of relationship has operated between rights in masculine mode and and emotional life in feminine mode. I believe that we have reached the limits of a historical impasse of this sort. Now that they are a little freer perhaps, a little more autonomous maybe, women today have to make the move from subjective claims to an affirmation of objective rights appropriate to them; and rights are always, for citizens, accompanied by duties.

Women must make the move from the *affidamento* or trust accorded to one person, to committing themselves to an explicitly proposed objective programme. This latter is decisive at the European level since many diverse subjectivities are being called upon to enter into a dialogue and to vote. If the proposals are elaborated solely in terms of a subjective process – Italian, for example, – it is hard to make them understood by and to share them with women of other countries and other cultures. A humble gesture of non-nationalistic claiming

Democracy Begins Between Two

of rights will therefore be to accept making proposals in words that can be shared by all women and men. Even men, after all, are required to vote through rights for women!

This real difficulty in passing from simple subjectivity to objectivity should not hide behind the call for quotas for participation in political power. Democracy cannot be confused with power unless it is that of each man and woman. So, in my view, one cannot demand 50/50 parity in representation at the political level without first of all demanding the right to responsibility towards the self and the community for each woman and each man.

A similar difficulty in developing a new form of objectivity for women can also be seen at the most everyday level. I'll give one example of this. A few weeks ago I was asked by one of you to give a talk in the context of a certain programme and I had agreed to this programme. Yesterday I learned that the programme had changed. This way of operating is not, in my view, democratic since I had said 'yes' to one thing, whereas something quite different was imposed on me at the last moment. Besides, this way of behaving gives rise to conflict, loss of identity and of coexistence between women.

So I find myself invited today, because of a change of programme, to be the first to speak, and to speak as a simple female citizen to three female members of parliament, whereas the initial proposal was that I should speak last, after two female members of parliament – Nilde Iotti and Livia Turco – to whom I could have suggested changes in the Constitution and the Civil Code from the perspective of my theory and practice of a politics of difference.

So I want to ask these three members of parliament their opinion on what priority should be given now to the juridical definition of rights which would protect the physical and moral inviolability of woman, her dignity, respect for her work as her own, even if it is intellectual; in other words, their opinion on the need, nowadays, to establish an objective form of protection, by means of positive rights, for the identity of each woman as a woman, and not as a neutral-abstract or masculine individual, nor even only as a mother.

In my view, women's liberation cannot develop without specific civil rights, and therefore sexed civil rights. I do not think that such rights can be defined in the face of existing civil codes: for example, by entrusting women juridically with a right to 'autonomy' or 'self-determination' only. This has very little meaning at the level of civil society. It is rather like granting the daughter subjective permission within a great national or supranational family built on a patriarchal model.

If men and women are now to deal with each other as equals, a civil identity for each gender, protected by objective rights, has to be defined.

The emphasis on 'self-determination', even though it represents an introductory training in autonomy, freedom and responsibility for women, is not enough to secure the framework or objective content of a civil code. Now, the limits of a subjectivity must be determined by an objectivity. This is necessary for investing an individual with a civil identity and for arbitrating relationships between individuals. It is particularly necessary in regulating relations between men and women since subjectivity and objectivity are, in that instance, double.

To set up a right to autonomy of choice in opposition to a right in masculine, so-called neutral, mode is inadequate as an emancipatory move to secure for women civil recognition equivalent to that of men. It remains a subjective demand which fails to sanction the objectivity of an identity, either for a woman or between women, or between ma(e)n and woma(e)n. It remains, in fact, nothing but a means of enslaving women to a juridical objectivity determined by and for men. All the problems concerning abortion, sexual violence – like rape, incest, assault, etc. – are proof of this: they lack a legal means of prevention appropriate to the two genders, and an appropriate form of penalization. So 'rape' is not a 'crime', as some European countries claim in an effort to sanction the act sufficiently; 'rape' is a particular way of violating an individual in their body, and in their private and public dignity.

Yet our civil codes lack a word for identifying the felony perpetrated, most often against women. The word is lacking, in my view, because the act touches the body insofar as it is linked with the spirit: it is not just

The Representation of Women

a matter of possessing the body of the other but of penetrating the sphere of their intimacy. Furthermore, it is a sexed felony, one which entails above all an infraction of the relations between individuals. This aspect of right is virtually absent from our civil codes, and it is particularly so where sex is involved. Sex, for the State as for the Church, should remain taboo, relegated to the family home – which has most certainly not helped to promote civil coexistence at this level!

In this way, women are not protected by the law as women and often, precisely for this reason, they do not report the violence they have been subjected to, because it remains 'private' violence, for which they lack the words to express themselves in a public, legal manner. Appropriate civil rights are necessary to protect the physical and moral integrity of women, that is, the inviolability of the individual. Rights of this kind, as well as making an explicit contribution towards dissuading the rapist, could assist women to affirm and to safeguard their own inviolability both insofar as it constitutes an individual right and insofar as it concerns respect for civil society as a whole.

Protecting women within the city boundaries is necessary, but it is perhaps even more so within the home. The number of women attacked by their husband or lover is scarcely believable. Yet they are considered under the power of the head of the family and the State does not want to know anything about them.

And the same is true for little girls, young girls and adolescent girls who are victims of incest on the part of the father or of another member of the family, incest which often leads to pregnancy for the older girls. Better to leave it as a family matter, people say, not to report it, unless the daughter, who is not yet of age as a juridical subject and who lacks both the economic independence and the authority with regard to the family to allow herself such a move, wishes to do so.

I wonder, and I am asking you, how we can possibly work democratically towards women's liberation while closing our eyes to violence of this kind directed at the body and dignity of women? Yet many women are opposed to sexed rights.

For some of them, it is a question of not drawing attention to the fact that women and men are not equal, from fear of losing advantages which they have already gained or, perhaps, through lack of awareness of their difference. For others, the law itself is rejected as an instrument of male power. But a civil society cannot be organized without laws, and witholding their definition in favour of women amounts, objectively, to colluding with the violence against them.

Once again, training in autonomy and self-determination is not enough to protect women juridically. The content of rights has, of necessity, to be relevant to both women and men, since the community is composed of both genders.

We run the risk of conflict and persecution if rights are affirmed solely in the name of subjectivity, in addition to the fact that it is impossible to regulate relationships between individuals belonging to different groups, particularly to different genders, in this way. Nor, moreover, should one confuse the apprenticeship in self-consciousness which has sometimes developed in the between-women, with women's access to civil identity and responsibility on an equal footing with men. Positing difference where it ought not to exist amounts to perpetuating the patriarchal culture which has kept women subservient to its laws.

At the European level, the need for a jurisprudence in favour of women is even more obvious since we find ourselves caught up in a mixture of customary laws which run the risk of causing women's autonomy to lose ground. And it is not enough to fight from time to time against rape – ethnic, for example, – sexual mutilation, etc. We have to define laws which anticipate offences and which prevent the constant falling back into the same crimes.

We have to define these for other women but also for ourselves, on pain of behaving like wealthy matriarchs who are by now secure in their own rights. The legislation which has yet to be defined for other women more often than not does not even exist for us. A duty which falls to us in our era is to discover and establish a new universality.

Gaining access to civil identity, inscribing corresponding positive rights in the codes and wanting to bring these about for ourselves and for all other women, is part of the work of women's liberation. This has priority as far as access to power is concerned. It is the first step towards democracy that has to be accomplished, and it remains the most crucial one. Exercizing representation in the name of feminine identity, without ensuring the right and duty of each woman legally at the civil level, is useless. It does not work today in a European country and it will be even less valid shortly in the European Union. Rights appropriate to the feminine gender, rights which serve to mediate in the exercise of such a function, are indispensable if women are to be democratically represented.

I fear that, unless this stage is achieved, women will become accomplices of an increase in authority and aggression which will not help the liberation of all women and even less of humanity. Quite the reverse!

Europe Captivated by New Myths

Poor Europe! How strange and barely rational the votes cast at the most recent European elections appear, particularly in Italy and France. They seem desperate, dictated by the logic of seduction rather than with the interests of male and female citizens at heart. The real winners are, in fact, money, the power of the media, fake novelty, things that are all the more avidly sought after by political life as we know it today since most party programmes lack any real content.

On Sunday 12 June, male and female citizens did not elect individuals worthy of their confidence to whom they could entrust their own needs and desires, except in a few regions like Emilia-Romagna. They voted, men and women, for the unknown quantity, for electoral promises, for media images and hype, if they did not abstain altogether. When they did choose to vote, they opted for 'distancing' that reality which they perceive as far from their own: Europe. They still have not grasped that they are Europe, that we are now Europeans, and

Article written for the newspaper 'The Daily', on the occasion of the results of the European elections (19 June 1994).

that declaring oneself for Europe means standing up and declaring oneself for each of us.

'Europe is far too distant a reality for me', an Italian female member of parliament declared in my face, and she added: 'All I expect from Europe is one big swindle'. She still has not understood that Europe depends, in part, on her political work, and has not even grasped that male Italian members of parliament, including those who belong to her own party or group, represent her in the framework of the European Parliament. Statements like hers reinforce and justify the ignorance of the average citizen concerning the European Union.

This kind of talk also fails to acknowledge the right to expression accorded to each of us, male and female, by the Treaty of Maastricht, particularly through a right of petition which each of us can address in his/her name to the President of the European Parliament, and through recourse to the Mediator.

The Treaty of Maastricht also opens up the possibility of a new definition of citizenship which would not be limited to a right to vote or to circulate freely on European territory. It involves a new approach to civil identity which concerns each and every one of us. I have begun working with Renzo Imbeni, an Emilian member of the European Parliament, on the statute of this citizenship.

The definition of a new European citizenship, favourable to each man and woman, requires a reinforcement of the specific rights of individuals so that they can accede to an enlarged community without being absorbed, annulled, annihilated. In this sense, the European Union can contribute to the development of a democratic process. It is essential, if this task is to be accomplished, that citizens, male and female, and not just capitalists and businessmen with an eye to a good deal, pay attention to the European Union.

But entering the European Union with a democratic objective requires giving up that form of everyday subjectivism which could, indeed, be called nationalism: 'Europe doesn't interest me, it doesn't belong to me, I'm Italian or French'. If European identity is to see to it that it does not entail a loss of human identity for each person, male and female, it must also attend to the conditions which permit coexistence between citizens belonging to different nations, traditions and cultures.

It is not possible to limit oneself, at the European level, to a purely subjective discussion, since debate and dialogue have to develop between very diverse subjectivities. We have to discover a new objectivity, in other words an objectivity which protects the lives of individuals, their uniqueness, but also coexistence between all the individuals who make up the European Union. It is only possible to hold discussions at the objective level, but I do not believe that objectivity can be reduced to an economic problem, a problem of money or of defence of the national territory.

*

The fact that everyone, male and female, has to eat, to have a roof over their head, to be dressed and educated is what objectivity means.

Protecting both our health and our happiness, which are two aspects of the same reality, is also an objective necessity; it is harder to be happy when we are ill, and it is not easy to achieve a good state of health without happiness. Both these values, which can be shared by all citizens, male and female, of Europe, depend on us looking after our environment: our air, our water, our food.

Another goal is to ensure peace and friendship amongst us. To achieve this, we have to learn new habits which respect both identity and sharing between men and women of our city, and coexistence between the races and cultures now present here or resident on European territory.

We must, moreover, bear in mind that work cannot be created if we despise the person who works, his/her living environment, nor if we despise coexistence amongst ourselves. So it is necessary to create a new type of work which respects human dignity and its basic values. I am thinking, for example, of employment in the service of the environment (a proposal put forward by Jacques Delors, President of the European Commission), of employment which develops natural resources without destroying them, of employment which fosters an increase in coexistence amongst us.

Europe Captivated by New Myths

Of course, I have made innovative proposals. But, in my view, political projects for Europe cannot simply imitate the past but, on the contrary, have to shoulder responsibility for the earth and the sun, for today and the future.

Appendix

I wanted the *Report on Citizenship of the Union* by Renzo Imbeni to be reproduced in my book to ensure that it would be remembered. In fact, the vote against it runs the risk of erasing this document from the archives of the European Parliament. Renzo Imbeni requested a vote of this sort out of political integrity. I wanted, therefore, to salute his gesture and to safeguard the traces of his work.

Report on Citizenship of the Union by Renzo Imbeni

A.
PROPOSAL FOR RESOLUTION

The European Parliament

– in the light of its resolutions of 14 June 1991 on European citizenship (GU n. C 183 of 15.7.1991, p. 473), of 21 November 1991 on citizenship of the Union (GU n. C 236 of 16.12.1991, p. 205), of 18 November 1992 on European policy on immigration (GU n. C 337 of 21.12.1992, p. 94), of 19 November 1992 on the abolition of internal frontier controls and on the free circulation of individuals within the European Community (GU n. C 337 of 21.12.1992, p. 211), of 11 March 1993 on respect for human rights in the European Community (Annual Report of the European Parliament) (GU n. C 115 of 26.4.1993, p. 178), and of 21 April 1993 on the recrudescence of racism and xenophobia in Europe and the danger of extreme right-wing violence (GU n. C 150 of 31.5.1993, p. 127),

– in the light of arts. F, 8, 8 A-E, 138 D and E, K1 of the Treaty of European Union,

– in the light of the declarations of the European Council of Birmingham of 16 October 1992,
– in the light of the Conference of the Economic and Social Committee on a Citizens' Europe of 27 and 28 September 1993,
– in the light of article 148 of its regulations,
– in the light of the Report of the Commission for Public Freedom and Internal Affairs and of the opinions of the Commission for Institutional Affairs and of the Commission for Women's Rights (A3–0437/93),
A. considering that the notion of citizenship as defined in article 8 of the Treaty represents an important stage in the process of the democratic construction of the political Union of the European Community insofar as it postulates an active role for citizens of the member states within the community system,
B. emphasizing its commitment and determination to see to it that, as recommended by the articles of the Treaty of Maastricht relating to citizenship, it be applied rapidly and accurately; and that it be situated in the perspective of citizenship relating to a European entity organized and structured on the basis of a constitution as the appropriate legislative framework for the definition of the rights and duties of citizens of the Union.
C. bearing in mind that attributing such rights and duties to citizens of the Union expresses the political will in the making of member states to amplify the notion of citizenship and to confer on it a dimension which would be in keeping with the present structure

of European society – multicultural, multi-ethnic and multireligious – and which requires rules of coexistence based on positive norms,

D. bearing in mind that cultural plurality poses anew the problem of individual freedom and points to the need for recognition of and respect for the difference between women and men as the basis of democratic union between citizens, nations and cultures,

E. observing however that, since the status of citizen of the Union is subordinate to the beneficiary's belonging to one of the member states, it follows paradoxically as a result of positive right that the Union recognizes that certain individuals have rights without being able to intervene in determining the conditions for acquiring, enjoying and forfeiting such rights,

F. considering that participation in political and social life by male and female citizens of the Union, as indeed by male and female citizens of other countries resident in the European Union, is hindered in member states by a large number of laws and regulations and that one of the tasks facing member states should be to get rid of such obstacles,

G. noting that the automatic connection between citizenship of the Union and that of a member state does not aim to exclude citizens of other countries normally resident within the Union from the generality of rights and duties of the community citizen, since this would go against the idea of a Union accessible to the individual as such and undermines the protection of the fundamental rights of such citizens,

H. emphasizing that the adoption of the Charter of the rights and duties of citizens of other countries within the Union sought by Parliament is therefore particularly urgent,

I. taking care to specify that community duties and rights will be valid and effective when it is possible to have the principles of a Constitutional Charter of the Union as reference;

J. bearing in mind that citizenship of the Union should be defined autonomously on the basis of the principles and the politico-institutional arrangement outlined by the future constitution,

K. firmly convinced that coherent action in constructing citizenship is essential if a higher degree of European integration – an indispensable condition of accelerated unification and democratization of community institutions – is to be attained,

L. emphasizing that the process of implementing citizenship of the Union should mean a greater guarantee of effective enjoyment of the right to work, to dignified living conditions (minimum wage, health care, right to accommodation) and to protection of the environment for the citizens of member states,

Citizenship of the Union and the Treaty Currently in Force

1. welcomes the new dispositions on European citizenship contained in the Treaty of Maastricht but deplores that many of the requests for the defining of citizens'

Report on Citizenship of the Union

rights and duties put forward by the European Parliament *have not been taken into consideration*;

2. argues that the right of the citizen of the Union to an active and passive vote in local and European elections in the member state of residence represents a noteworthy innovative element and, therefore, requests the Council, the Commission and the administrations of the member states that regulations concerning the exercise of such rights become effective from 1 January 1994 for European elections and from 28 February 1994 for local elections;

3. in this connection draws attention to the fact that effective access for citizens of the Union to the status of active and passive voters in their state of residence requires the definition of *common criteria* for certain aspects such as:

— the notion of residence,
— the notion of domicile,
— regulating the alternation between exercising the right to vote in the country of residence or in that of origin as regards European elections, and therefore requests the Commission — as it has already done with its own resolutions concerning the European elections — to *define* such criteria *clearly* in its proposals;

4. recommends member states to establish within the deadline the dispositions necessary for the application of art. 8C of the Treaty, but in this connection takes care to specify the limits set out by this article insofar as the diplomatic protection guaranteed to citizens is not

of a community nature, but has rather a 'reciprocal' character;

5. reiterates that the right to petition and the right to have recourse to the mediator represent an enrichment of the system of guaranteeing individual rights and wishes to point out that, since such rights are not exclusive to citizens of the Union, their sphere of application *leaves out of consideration* the nationality of the citizen; considers that the reinforcement of the transparency of community acts and the right of citizens to be aware of those which concern them is a condition of the functioning of the aforementioned institutes;

6. envisages the right of all citizens legally resident in the Union to circulate freely within the territory of member states as having immediate effect and, in this respect, refers to the resolutions adopted on this subject;

7. requests the Commission, before the revision of the Treaty, to draw up a proposal recommending member states to bring recognition of citizenship – based on uniform criteria – into force for citizens of other countries resident on the territory of the Union;

European Citizenship within a European Union Perspective

8. proposes that citizenship of the Union should have as its goal its own autonomy based on the politico-institutional arrangement set out by the European Constitution;

9. therefore deems it necessary that, at the next Intergovernmental Conference, or in the other bodies to be appointed by the revision of the Treaty, timely modifi-

cations should be made, hopefully by procedures which are more democratic than those which preceded the Maastricht Agreement, with the aim of integrating the following positive rights inherent in the identity of the individual into citizenship of the Union. It goes without saying that such rights apply in their virtual entirety to all individuals as fundamental and universal rights and for this very reason should figure in the text of the European Constitution

a) the right to work, to parity of opportunity and to dignified working conditions,
b) the right of young people to study, to culture, to education,
c) the right to a healthy environment and to respect for health,
d) the right of all before the law to the juridical recognition of their identity as subjects of right, men and women, as the premise of an effective application of the principle of equality and non-discrimination,
e) the right to the physical and moral inviolability of the individual,
f) the right to active and passive voting in European elections throughout the Union irrespective of the member state of residence of the citizen,
g) the right to information concerning the activity of the institutions of the Union with the aim of guaranteeing their transparency and accessibility to citizens,
h) the right to have recourse to the Mediator, individually or through representative associations or with

public juridical aid, even in cases of violation of fundamental rights and that the Mediator should be able to have recourse to the Court of Justice,
i) the right of all professions to circulate freely and of all member states to have access to public office,
j) the right of citizens of other countries who normally reside within the Union to acquire citizenship of it, on certain conditions,

10. deems it necessary to proceed to the introduction of a community norm which, taking the various cultures and traditions present in the states of the Union into account, would protect such rights inherent in the individual as, for example, for women full self-determination and responsibility in all fields of private and public life, by overriding the residual juridical norms of patriarchal stamp still present in the legislations of many member states;
11. holds that the practices currently followed in certain member states to guarantee citizens of other countries resident on their territory the right to vote in European and other elections should be fully respected and safeguarded in future agreements concerning electoral procedures for elections to the European Parliament;
12. requests the Commission
– to draft a European Civil Code based on the bill for the Constitution of the Union which the Parliament is about to adopt and, from the harmonization of some material, civil codes for individual states so that citizens

of the Union may enjoy an initial group of homogeneous juridical rights of situation;
– to draw up as indicated above proposals for the harmonization of juridical competence and coming of age;
– to propose a revision of its own resources in order to create a fiscal system in the Union which would represent a guarantee of transparency for the citizen concerning his contribution to the administration of the Union;
13. invites the Commission of the Community to propose, particularly in the sectors indicated by the Treaty, a policy for the Union on immigration, taking into account the need fully to respect fundamental rights and to avoid unjust discrimination against foreign residents;
14. in conformity with article K6 of the Treaty of Union recommends the Council
– to create a European civil service and subsequently to organize a common European defence as set out in the Treaty of Union,
– to introduce the institution of the referendum into community law both as consultative, that is before an act is adopted and as constitutive, that is to confirm the validity and effectiveness of a decision by member states,
– to adopt a decision which would sanction in community law the existence of a flag and hymn for the Union,
15. requests its President to transmit the present resolution to the Council, the Commission, the Economic

and Social Committee, the governments and parliaments of the member states and of countries applying for membership.

B.
JUSTIFICATION

General considerations

1. The notion of European citizenship is both old and new in the community dynamic.
Already in the Treaty of Rome certain rights, whose beneficiaries were the citizens of member states, were specified. Subsequently at the Paris Summit of 1974, heads of state and government took certain 'special rights', to be granted to their citizens, into consideration.
The same can be said concerning the protection of the fundamental rights of community citizens which have a juridical basis in numerous articles of the EEC Treaty (arts. 2, 7, 48, 51, 42–66, 119, 173 and 177).
In reality, the entire community system is based on the protection of individual rights even though, since community legislation does not replace that of member states, it is not primarily the business of the Community and its present institutional structures to guarantee individual citizens complete protection of fundamental rights.
Nonetheless it is worth noting once more that the

aforementioned articles are of a *purely economic* nature and scope.

2. With the Treaty of Maastricht we are, on the contrary, present at the formal birth of 'citizenship of the Union' and are obliged to make a fundamental change of course in imposing 'European citizenship'. In practice, we are in the presence of a process of transformation of the subjective juridical position of the individual in community legislation.

The political and juridical scope of the expression 'citizenship of the Union' as it figures in the Treaty of Maastricht is moreover emphasized. On the political level one cannot fail to note how 'European citizenship' means the abandoning of a purely economic European construction insofar as citizens are no longer mere targets of community norms but become protagonists in the dynamic process of constructing Europe and community activity, a process which already impinges on their lives and will do so increasingly. On the juridical level, it is important to note that certain individual juridical situations, precisely because they are recognized as relating to a citizen of the Union, can no longer be considered as 'purely internal situations' and thus beyond the scope of application of the Treaty. It is clear moreover that citizenship of the Union will impinge in a more punctual way on the juridical position of individuals.

3. The Treaty of Rome, as it emerges modified by the Unique Act, sets out two types of freedom as regards the citizen of the European Community: freedom of circulation and non-discrimination.

The first is regulated by arts. 48 and 50 (freedom of circulation for salaried and non-salaried workers); the second by arts. 7, 48, 119 and 220 (prohibition of discrimination on the grounds of nationality and sex).

This regulation is under the control of the Commission and of the Court of Justice.

It is, moreover, given its programmatic character, specified by means of secondary norms such as regulations and directives which ensure that it operates in the economic and social world resulting from the community construction thus far achieved.

4. We can cite

– EEC regulation no.1612 of 15.10.1968 relating to the freedom of circulation of workers within the community;

– EEC regulation no.1251/70 of 29.6.1970 relating to the right of workers to remain resident on the territory of a member state after they have worked there;

– Council directive (90/335/EEC) of 28.6.1990 relating to the right of salaried and non-salaried workers to remain resident when they have ceased their professional activity;

– Council directive (90/366/EEC) of 28.6.1990 relating to students' right of residence.

Freedoms of this sort were conceived to guarantee citizens, defined as economic subjects, the possibility of movement but only as long as their transfer from one member state to the another does not create new economic difficulties for the latter.

Thus the community citizen is individualized as a

Report on Citizenship of the Union

productive factor and not in his/her more complex dimension as an individual participating in the economic, social, political, etc. worlds.

5. The Treaty of Maastricht instituted citizenship of the Union. Art. B states: 'The union is determined to reinforce the protection of the rights and interests of the citizens of its member states by means of the institution of a citizenship of the Union'.

Art. 8, of Title II, defines as citizens of the Union 'whoever has citizenship of a member state'.

6. The citizen, since he belongs to the community, gains new rights:
— the right of those resident in a member state different from their state of origin to vote in and to be eligible for local and European elections;
— diplomatic and consular protection granted to community citizens by the authorities of other member states;
— the right to petition and to have recourse to the mediator;
— the reaffirming of the right to freedom of circulation: art. 8A refers to the citizen understood as such and no longer, as in the Treaty of Rome, as an economic subject.

7. This is a first step towards the recognition and protection, at the level of community regulation, of political and civil rights.

As regards the modalities for acquiring citizenship of the Union, these are determined by national ones. Thus any modification of criteria specific to national regulations will have direct consequences on citizenship of the Union.

In the course of intergovernmental conferences the Commission had put forward the proposal that each state should adopt a unilateral declaration on the notion of nationality so that the influence of the institution of citizenship of the Union on the regulations of member states be reinforced.

The Conference, wishing to maintain intact the national sovereignty of each state in this matter, did not adopt this proposal.

The Spanish delegation also had introduced an innovative proposal on this topic: to make possible the extension of rights and duties, deriving from status as European citizen, to those who do not enjoy citizenship of a member state.

The automatic connection between citizenship of the Union and that of a member state places those who come from other countries radically beyond the reach of the nascent corpus of rights and duties which will be attributed to community citizens.

The Treaty of Maastricht considers those who come from other states either in relation to the controls which they undergo when they cross the external frontiers of the Union or in relation to the norms which will be adopted by the Council on Conditions of Employment.

The right to petition the European Parliament (art. 138D) and the right to have recourse to the Mediator (art. 138E) constitute the only new elements.

The Treaty of Maastricht, in force since November 1st

Report on Citizenship of the Union

1993, must be fully and rapidly implemented. The European Parliament will see to this. It is very important that, from this very moment, the next modifications, outlined by the same Treaty for 1996, should be planned, in the context of the Intergovernmental Conference, with the aim of realizing a true European Union as was affirmed in the draft for the Treaty of Union, drawn up by the European Parliament on the initiative of Mr Spinelli.

The Nationality – Citizenship Relationship

8. The relationship between nationality and citizenship is becoming increasingly diversified.

The level of personal mobility, both within the Community and in relations with other countries, is steadily increasing.

Some community countries like the United Kingdom, France, the Netherlands, Belgium, as ex-colonial countries, have long recognized the phenomenon of immigration; others, like Germany, recognized this phenomenon more recently for largely economic reasons.

The collapse of the two blocks, which had in fact hindered people from Eastern Europe from circulating freely, put an end to this situation.

9. The constantly expanding globalization of the economy leads not only to millions of people being on the move but also produces effects on the economic and social structures of many countries: decisions are often taken which are beyond their control. In addition, we are witnessing massive movements of people in search

of even minimal conditions of subsistence. These factors mean that the relationship between State and individual can no longer be interpreted as it was in the past. The individual is no longer, only, either the citizen with his baggage of rights-duties or the foreigner cut off from the specific civil and political relations of the collectivity. Nationality has taken shape, above all in European states, in relation to *ius sanguinis* and *ius soli*.

It was then enriched by the religious, linguistic, traditional, etc. rights which characterized the community. These elements did not give rise to friction, within the latter, as long as nationality and citizenship corresponded perfectly. Nowadays on the contrary, the dimension of citizenship can no longer be squeezed into that of nationality on the same grounds as used to obtain.

The presence of millions of immigrants, above all from the third world, who actively participate in the economic life of our countries, makes the adoption of an adequate concept of citizenship necessary.

10. It should have as its basis what has been built up by the community but with the aim of going beyond this.

The resolution of the European Parliament on citizenship of the Union (GU n. C 326 of 16.12.1991) affirms: '... citizenship of the Union should be defined autonomously in such a way as to create a genuine status for citizens'.

'... Moreover the institution of citizenship involves the fixing by law of a system of social rights'.

Report on Citizenship of the Union

11. It will be our task to put forward such proposals once more bearing in mind that they were formulated by the European Parliament with the aim of being approved by the new Treaty. Now that this has been ratified the new juridical framework has to be borne in mind if we are to go beyond it.

Thus the aim of this report, if it is to be useful and not repetitive, is to indicate objectives relating to:

a) implementing the Treaty of Maastricht;
b) revising the Treaty, outlined in 1996;
c) approval of the European Constitution (which must create a homogeneous juridical framework out of the polymorphousness of the present one where local decision-making procedures coexist with intergovernmental ones). The point of reference of our discussion is the project for a European Constitution which the institutional commission is drawing up.
d) creation of a European Civil Code on the basis of a harmonization, in a specified range of subjects, of the Civil Codes of individual states.

Towards a Codification of the Rights of Citizenship

12. The rights of citizens are to be defined in positive terms and no longer only through the protection of economic or civil interests effected by the codes. The citizen of the Union is not only an economic subject, and thus the totality of his being is to be represented in positive right in such a way as to favour the structuring of social relations based on the reciprocal recognition of individuals.

Democracy Begins Between Two

13. A series of factors in contemporary Western society makes the positive definition of rights increasingly urgent.

Our societies have become multi-ethnic, multicultural, multi-religious, phenomena which drive in the direction of the creation of rules enabling coexistence not only on the basis of definition in the negative of one's own and the other's freedom (the non-interference in one's personal sphere of the other) but in a positive sense, reinforcing the civil identity of individuals as such. Thus even cultural plurality poses anew the problem of individual freedom and points to the need for respect for difference between women and men as the foundation of a democratic union between citizens, nations and cultures. The creation of a wider and, above all, juridically recognized sphere of subjectivity based on new positive norms is necessary. This has, as its consequence and as premise, an extensive redefinition of the man-woman relationship. The latter has, in fact, changed radically in our societies in recent decades and requires juridical recognition.

14. A specific contribution to reflection on this theme is offered by the assessments contained in a draft code of citizenship signed by Luce Irigaray and by the reporter. This draft notes amongst other things that: 'The lack of legislation appropriate to women can be seen today in various ways: in particular in the scandals and trials concerning the violence of which they are victims. National civil codes as well as constitutions and the *Universal Declaration of Human Rights* all lack terms

relating to specific rights which would enable such crimes to be judged. Thus rape is defined as a crime and not as rape, which fails to protect the woman as such and leaves the ordinary citizen unaware of the felony he commits when he rapes someone. The same is true as regards the freedom to choose to be a mother which is defined, at its best, as permission to have an abortion without penal consequences: such a formulation of the law reveals its complicity with patriarchal power which retains the right to legislate over a woman's body, even if she is of age. Women even lack rights relating to the custody of their children, especially in the case of intercultural marriages, to a culture appropriate to their identity (for example, rights prohibiting sexual mutilation), to their physical or symbolic representation in public places, etc. As long as such rights are lacking, crimes involving women are considered almost exclusively in the penal context which does not promote civil peace. What is more, no preventive legislation exists: one which would entrust a woman with responsibility for herself as a citizen and which, by considering her as a civil individual, would give the community the responsibility of preventing the crimes involving her, involving both of them.

Often clauses are added to civil codes, to constitutions and to the *Universal Declaration of Human Rights*, particularly at the request of women, which testify to the fact that the issues are not being dealt with exhaustively. On the other hand, when there is a clash of arguments, these are often expressed in too abstract and general a manner for each male and female citizen to be able to interpret and practise them. So law becomes a matter for experts in national and international jurisdiction. It no longer has the function of constituting and regulating a civil community made up of male and female citizens responsible for themselves and for the community. This lack is aggravated by the fact that legislation expresses itself in terms of the right to "have", to satisfy needs and desires, to possess (including possession of one's own body understood as a good), rather than in terms of responsibility before oneself and before others as civil individuals'.

The differences should not lead to equality understood as seeking parity with a dominant model but to a consideration of their specific characteristics which are not referable to anything else.

The multicultural and multi-ethnic dimension of our community requires us to rethink the rules of coexistence which were founded on positive norms created by national communities that were not, originally, open ones.

The reorganization of rights will be conceived on a supranational basis, attributing rights that are not linked with a precise ethnic, religious, etc. identity so that social relations can be regulated without presenting elements of non-integration again. The construction of the Union requires the definition of new rights and duties which will guarantee civil coexistence between the races (even in the context of the family), between the sexes (even from different traditions), between the different generations and cultures.

15. The new Constitution of the Union, which the European Parliament is drawing up, will define the politico-institutional framework on the basis of which the harmonization of the civil codes of the member states is to be completed. In this way citizens who live on community territory will be offered homogeneous juridical situations as far as positive rights are concerned and thus the occurrence of less protected situations within one or more member state will be avoided.

Considering that young people are taking an increasingly precocious part in social life, it is appropriate to grant them an identity of their own which is not dependent on the legitimization offered by parents, and at a younger age.

The Constitution of the Union must make provision for the right to work, valid protection of the environment and the guarantee of dignified living conditions to citizens.

16. Parallel with the positivization of such rights, it is essential that community citizens be provided with duties which really integrate them into the Community on the same basis as the integration offered by the national context.

One of the first duties which characterize citizenship is fiscal obligation. The system of personal resources has to be modified so that an easily individualizable share of resources goes directly into the Union's funds, thus giving the citizen a clear picture of how much he contributes to the running of community institutions, and creating a direct relationship between citizen and supranational authority.

Since the Treaty of Maastricht sees to the instituting of a foreign policy and of a common defence policy, provision should be made for participation in a common army.

It would be appropriate to plan the instituting of a civil service of the Union on an experimental basis.

Conclusions

17. The first requirement is to implement the provisions made by the Treaty of Maastricht as regards the right to an active and passive vote in European elections from 1994 and in local ones from the second semester of 1994.

18. On the basis of what has been set out above, it is proposed that the intergovernmental Conference, planned by the Treaty of Maastricht for 1996, in order to assist with the modifications that will be necessary, should examine the following proposals and assess how to insert them in the Treaty:

A. Citizenship of the Union is to be defined autonomously on the basis of the principles and of the politico-institutional arrangement provided for by the Constitution;

B. the right to be citizens of the Union, even for residents who are not citizens of a member state, should be provided for, in specific circumstances;

Report on Citizenship of the Union

C. the introduction into the Treaty on Union of positive rights for community citizens on the basis of the recognition of differences and of the civil identity of individuals as such;

D. harmonization of the age of maturity should go ahead;

E. the Union should adopt measures enabling citizenship of the Union to correspond to effective enjoyment of the right to work, to the protection of the environment and to dignified living conditions;

F. the Union should reaffirm the primacy of community right over that of member states, as maintained by the draft for a Constitution of the Union.

G. the Union should make every effort to harmonize the civil codes of member countries in matters concerning the positive rights to be attributed to citizens with the aim of adopting a European civil code;

H. a fiscal system which places the citizen in direct relation to the administrative organization of the Union should be finalized;

I. until there exists a common defence system, an equivalent civil service should be created capable of backing up the military one, once this has been created;

J. the introduction of an identity document for resident citizens, to replace the existing ones, should be planned; work towards producing this should begin soon so that it will be completed by the time that the Constitution of the Union comes into force.

Notes

1. Movement founded by Gisèle Halimi which is involved with 'women's issues', for example problems concerning the right to abortion.
2. With me were: Adriana Cavarero, Renzo Imbeni, Antonio La Forgia and Livia Turco.
3. Henceforth the *Report* appears as *R.* and the *Draft Report* (which corresponds to the first, unamended version of the *Report*) as *D.R.*. The *Report on Citizenship of the Union*, by Renzo Imbeni, appears in *Appendix*.
4. In France the term used is 'equality' not 'parity' of opportunity.

Index

abortion, 30–1, 33, 43, 180, 211
absolute, 47, 124, 138
abstract, 9, 15, 26, 37, 51, 54, 57, 59, 63, 72–6, 82, 115, 154–5, 159, 170, 173, 179, 211
abuse, 84, 86
affidamento, 177
alienate/alienation, 42, 50, 52, 66, 70, 96, 99–101, 126, 137–8, 150, 166–7
Aristotle, 113

Beauvoir, Simone de, 122–3, 125–7
becoming, 4, 13, 16, 36, 43, 59, 131, 134, 154, 164, 166, 170
Berlinguer, Enrico, 2, 10, 106, 108, 110
between, 9, 13–14, 16, 22, 26, 120, 139, 148, 161, 170, 173, 180, 183
biology, viii, 30, 36, 83

body, 5, 8, 18, 26, 28, 30, 31–3, 36, 42, 44, 47, 52, 56, 71–2, 86, 99, 114, 131, 133, 170, 180–2, 211
Bologna, 21–22, 29, 60, 77, 108, 118
Buber, Martin, 128
Buddha, 115

caress, 114, 140
child/children, 32, 52, 56–7, 60, 86, 88–9, 95, 98, 104, 107, 125, 161, 171
Church, 18, 41, 43, 52, 100, 133, 160, 181
citizen/citizenship, 8, 9, 11–12, 14, 16–19, 23, 32, 38–9, 42, 51–9, 60–94, 118–20, 134, 154–5, 158, 162, 171, 174, 176, 185–6, 193–215
civil, x, 5, 9–13, 19, 28, 36, 39, 42, 45, 49–59, 60–94, 97, 99–100, 133, 155, 160–1, 171, 174–5, 179, 181

civilised/civilisation, 2, 12, 25–6, 31, 49, 54, 84, 103, 154, 163
CNRS, xi, 119
code, 16, 68; civil, 8–10, 12, 27, 31–2, 38, 43, 58, 60–94, 101, 134, 161, 163, 175, 179–80, 200, 209, 213; Draft Code of Citizenship, 61–73, 76, 87–8, 210; Penal, 10, 38, 67–8
coexistence, ix–x, 2, 5, 9–13, 16, 22, 24, 27, 46, 49–59, 63, 65, 68–9, 97, 99–100, 112, 117, 129, 155, 160–1, 163, 171–2, 178, 187–8, 195, 210, 212
communication, 9, 68, 115
communism, 2, 107–9
community, 8, 10, 24, 26, 37, 39, 45, 50, 51–9, 60–94, 98, 101, 132–3, 148, 154–5, 157, 163, 166, 170, 173, 175, 212
conflict, 8, 12–13, 32, 37, 54, 62, 66, 68, 84, 90, 158, 161, 178, 182
consciousness, 3, 4, 6, 163
couple, 24, 26, 36, 40, 43, 45, 68, 76, 96, 104, 160
culture, vii, 2–4, 6–8, 11, 13, 16, 25, 28, 29, 34, 36, 41, 43, 49, 50–60, 68, 74, 89, 96, 100, 115, 117, 119, 122, 128, 131, 136, 139, 141, 142–55, 160, 163, 172, 195, 199, 210, 212
custody, 32, 60, 71, 86, 89, 211

Delors, Jacques, 61, 157, 168, 188
democracy, 2, 11, 16, 22–32, 34, 38–9, 41, 65, 70, 74–5, 77, 79–80, 90, 100, 108, 118–20, 128, 130, 133, 163, 170, 172, 174, 177–8, 182, 187, 193–215
desire, 19, 33, 35–6, 72, 145, 165, 171, 185; for possession, 7, 111; sexual, 4, 56, 113
difference, 5, 7–10, 12–14, 16–17, 24, 26–7, 30, 33, 42, 47, 54, 59, 66, 74, 79–81, 87, 90–1, 96, 101, 103–4, 113–4, 117, 121–41, 125–6, 129, 133, 150–2, 161, 172, 176, 182–3, 187, 212
duty, 10, 74, 174–5, 177, 183, 194, 196, 212

economic, 3, 18, 34–5, 46, 50, 54–5, 58–9, 65–6, 76–7, 82–3, 102–3, 119, 132, 145–6, 148, 151, 156, 159–60, 162, 168, 182, 187, 202, 204–5, 207–9
ecstasy, 116
education, 1, 9, 16, 32, 59, 78,

Index

108, 142, 144–5, 153–5, 199
Emilia Romagna, 1, 19
environment, 8, 15, 75, 89, 152, 154, 157–9, 169, 188, 196, 199
equal/equality, 4, 11, 24, 27, 34, 76, 79, 82, 90–1, 107, 122, 127, 132–3, 142–55, 212; Commission for Equal Opportunities, 1, 19
equivalent, 1, 11–12, 90, 140, 143, 150, 180
ethics/ethical, 13, 24, 124, 130, 139–41
ethnic, 13, 49, 54, 67, 183, 195, 212
Europe, 12, 14, 17–18, 32, 49–50, 60–94, 97–8, 118–9, 143, 156–64, 176–7, 183, 185–9, 193–215; European Court of Justice, 204; European Parliament, 21–2, 207–9
excess, 104
exploit/exploitation, 3–4, 13, 107, 150–2

family, 5, 31, 36, 52–9, 66–8, 70–1, 95–105, 110, 146, 155, 160–1, 177, 181–2
father, 71, 112, 117, 131, 133, 182
female, vii, 5, 12, 18, 23, 38, 83, 112–3, 129, 131, 135, 142–55
feminine, vii–viii, 14, 30–2, 35–6, 38, 47, 73, 84, 90, 95, 100, 154, 172, 176–7; grammatical gender, 116, 121, 124, 149
feminism/feminist, 35, 37, 46, 125–6, 149
FGCI, xi, 77, 118
France, 12, 32, 36, 55, 63, 87, 92, 142–55, 175, 185
free/freedom, 2, 10, 29–31, 51, 60, 71, 74, 80, 89, 91, 97, 100, 107, 166–7, 180, 195, 203–4, 211
Freud, 126–7
future, 8, 23, 29, 41, 76, 95–6, 110, 152, 154–6, 163, 166, 188

gender, vii–ix, 5–7, 11–12, 14, 16–18, 26, 34, 36, 68, 76, 81, 83, 90, 96, 100, 114, 119, 125, 138–40, 143, 149–152, 179–80, 182–3; grammatical, see under feminine, masculine
genealogy, 36, 96, 129, 131
generation, 5, 7–9, 11, 53–4, 58, 66–8, 212
God, 6, 25, 57, 65, 67, 69, 72, 82, 134, 156–8, 160–1, 169
goods, 18, 25, 57, 65, 67, 69,

72, 82, 134, 156–8, 160–1, 169
govern/government, 23, 26, 76, 83, 99, 101, 103, 155, 172
Gramsci, Antonio, 2

happiness, 22, 25, 28, 47, 96, 104, 106, 108–10, 116, 120, 161, 165–73, 188
health, 75, 131, 159, 165–73, 188, 196, 199
Hegel, 27, 58, 139
History, 3, 5, 7–9, 13, 18, 22–3, 27–9, 34–5, 41, 43, 46, 50, 57, 68, 77, 95, 99, 102, 117, 140, 162–3, 168
horizontal, 47, 53–4, 96, 138

ideal, 7–8, 27–8, 34, 100, 106, 116, 124, 128–9, 171
identity, 4, 6, 12–14, 18, 28, 49, 51–2, 54, 58, 65–9, 79, 84, 97–8, 103–4, 114, 121–41, 159, 163, 179–80, 186–8, 199; women's, 2, 3, 30–6, 71, 80–3, 85–6, 96, 99, 121–41, 149, 150–1, 154, 178, 183–4
image, 6, 131
Imbeni, Renzo, 16, 19, 21–2, 24, 26, 28–9, 47, 49, 60–1, 63, 73, 76, 79, 80, 89, 91, 93, 109, 118, 120, 186, 193–215; Report by, 73–94, 192–215
individual, 9, 11, 13, 23, 25–6, 28, 37, 46, 50, 52, 56, 58–94, 97–8, 100, 104, 118, 124, 132–4, 156–8, 160, 162–3, 170, 174, 176, 180–1, 195, 199, 202, 204–5, 208–9
industrialisation, 4, 159

Irigaray, Luce, 22, 63, 118, 142, 210; works by: *I Love To You*, 21, 26, 41–2, 47, 60, 110–1, 115, 117–8, 125, 153, 165; *Je, Tu, Nous*, 131, 153; *Sexes and Genealogies*, 131, 152; *Speculum*, 47, 124–5, 131, 137; *Thinking the Difference*, 131, 153; *This Sex Which Is Not One*, 131; *To Be Two*, 106, 109–10, 114–5, 117–8, 140
irreducible, 26, 47, 104, 129, 139, 150
Italy, 12, 22, 40–1, 52, 63, 87, 97, 143, 176–7, 185

just/justice, 46, 83, 118, 120, 132, 143, 171

language, vii–x, 9, 15, 19, 32, 34–5, 47, 72, 75, 92, 100, 114, 124, 131, 135–7, 140, 144, 152–5, 208, 211;

Index

discourse, 9, 19, 32, 132; words, 28, 116, 128, 178–80
law, 6, 43, 72, 96, 101–2, 119, 133, 143, 162, 175, 181–4, 193–215, 211–12; common, 68; customary, 5, 63, 75, 183; penal, 8, 69, 72
Left, 93, 102, 170; Italian, 2, 48
Levinas, Emmanuel, 128
liberation, 11, 13, 101, 107, 109, 130, 132, 140, 184; women's, 2–3, 14, 30–1, 35, 39, 43, 64, 88, 90, 92, 95, 98, 107–8, 117, 132, 142, 172, 175–6, 179, 182–4
life, 57, 107–8, 155, 160, 163, 168, 173
love, 3, 5, 8, 16, 21, 25–8, 32, 35–6, 42–3, 45, 47, 67, 106–20, 124, 134, 138, 140, 166

male, vii, 5, 12, 18, 23, 112–3, 122, 129, 182
man/men, viii, 4, 6, 7, 10, 12–13, 16, 21–4, 26–9, 39, 42, 56, 63, 66, 95, 103, 107, 113, 118, 143, 152–3, 161
Marx/Marxism, 27, 46, 90, 107, 151
masculine, vii–viii, 1, 14, 31, 33–4, 37–8, 47, 73, 128, 134, 154, 172, 176–7, 179, 180; grammatical gender, 81, 83, 92, 116, 121, 124, 149
master-slave, 43, 58, 103, 162
maternity, 31–2, 43, 60, 67, 71, 89, 92, 100, 117, 131, 138, 143, 146, 211
media, 35, 159, 173, 185
mediate/mediation, 83, 116–7, 132, 153, 161–3, 173–4, 176; Mediator, 78, 198–200, 205
mother, 59, 112, 114, 135, 151, 176, 179

nation/national/nationalism, 3, 17, 49, 61–3, 66–7, 70, 81, 158, 162, 168, 177, 187, 204–5, 208, 212
natural, 3, 15, 43, 52–9, 65, 67–8, 89, 98–100, 176, 188; law, 38, 55
nature, 6, 7, 9, 13, 27–9, 43–4, 47, 101, 111–2, 114–5, 119, 128, 130–1, 139, 166, 168–9; state of, 42, 45, 49–59, 65–6, 83, 133
negate/negative/negativity, 17, 76, 83, 140
neutral, 9, 34, 37, 54, 59, 66, 80, 82, 98, 118, 124, 149–50, 155, 159, 170, 179–80

221

object/objective/objectivity, 10, 15, 83, 93, 116, 137, 171, 176–80, 187–8
one, 6, 15–16, 65, 70, 121–41, 159, 170–2
ONISEP, 145
other/Other, 3, 7–9, 12, 17, 26–7, 47, 57–8, 100, 111–12, 114–16, 119, 121–41, 152–3, 159, 166, 168–9

Paris Summit, 202
parity, 16, 17, 77, 82, 143, 178, 199
patriarchy, 31, 34–5, 54, 58, 71, 94, 117, 130, 183, 200
PCI, xi, 60
PDS, xi, 21–2, 40, 77, 160, 165
peace, 12, 31, 68, 72, 97, 188, 211
perceive/perception, 114–7, 139–40, 168
philosophy, 28, 121–41
Plato, 128–9
poetry, 2, 28
politics/political, 2, 5, 10, 13, 16, 18–9, 23, 28, 31–4, 37, 41, 43–4, 58, 62–3, 65, 69, 73–4, 88, 90, 96, 98, 102, 104, 108, 109, 118, 122, 124, 140–1, 143, 147, 158, 165–74, 185
positive, 2, 11, 31, 38, 69, 83, 90, 132, 166, 179, 195, 199, 209–10
possessions, 7, 9, 11, 24, 28–9, 58, 65, 67, 72, 103, 134, 161, 169, 181, 212
power, viii, 23, 32, 34–5, 39, 43–4, 46, 71, 98, 100–1, 104, 107, 118–9, 149, 162, 166–7, 172–4, 176, 178, 181–2, 184–5, 211
private, 3, 28, 33–4, 64, 66, 86, 94, 98, 108, 112, 117, 133, 165, 172, 180–1, 200
procreate, 36, 43, 57, 127
produce/production, 7, 13, 15, 23, 52, 107, 132, 158–9, 161, 163, 166–7
property, 8, 65, 67, 134
protect, 9, 18, 31, 56–7, 65–6, 71, 75, 101, 133–4, 162–3, 168, 173, 179, 181, 188, 196–7, 205
public, 3, 28, 32, 34, 36, 64, 71, 86, 94, 112, 117, 165, 172, 180, 200

race, 5, 7–9, 11, 53–4, 58–9, 63, 66, 67, 97, 101, 119, 122, 141, 163, 172, 176, 188, 212; racism, 46, 70, 156, 193
rape, 31, 71, 88, 180, 183, 211
rational/rationality, 59, 117, 122, 168, 185
rebirth, 29, 110–11

Index

refound, 22, 24–5, 98–9, 118, 161
relation/relationship, 3, 5, 8–11, 14–15, 17, 25–6, 39, 42, 47, 57, 59, 62–70, 97–9, 111–19, 126, 129, 132, 138, 140, 147, 152–9, 171–76, 180–3, 208, 210
religion/religious, 2, 3, 5, 24–5, 31, 42–3, 47, 54, 58, 66–7, 96, 99, 124, 131, 141, 160, 171, 195, 208, 212
representation, 32, 38, 71, 83, 89, 99, 101–2, 118, 131, 172, 174–84
reproduce, 52, 133, 177
respect, 8, 9, 12, 15–17, 32, 42, 47, 74, 80, 90–1, 112, 116–7, 119, 137, 154, 158, 161, 172
responsibility, 36, 43, 60–1, 64, 70–2, 84, 94–5, 99, 102, 133, 159–60, 171, 174–5, 178, 180, 183, 188, 200, 211–2
right(s), 10, 12, 36, 58, 60, 63, 67, 69, 71, 75, 78, 81, 86, 91–2, 102, 118, 132–3, 212; civil, 8, 10–11, 23, 30–1, 33, 38, 42–3, 56, 99–100, 161–2, 173–4, 179, 182, 194, 196, 199, 201–2, 205; sexed, 11, 47; Universal Declaration of Human, 38, 70–2, 134, 210–11;
women's, 14, 60, 79–91, 100, 133–4, 142–55, 174–84, 194
Right, 93, 160

salvation, 168–73
same, 114–5, 122, 127, 141, 151
Sartre, Jean-Paul, 114
secular, x, 10, 12, 160
self, 3, 9, 28, 36, 38, 43, 49, 51, 100, 104, 111–3, 116, 139, 141, 159, 168–70, 173, 175, 178, 212
sensation, 115
senses/sensibility, 5, 42, 59, 64, 115, 117, 139, 166, 170
sexed, 9, 11, 15, 47, 79, 89, 104, 118, 134, 136, 160, 179
sexism, 10, 46
singular/singularity, x, 9, 28, 57, 59, 66, 100, 102, 122, 127–8, 170
slavery, 43–7, 180
specific, 16, 36, 59, 69–70, 83, 86, 90, 132, 134, 145, 151, 155, 175, 187, 212
spirit/spiritual, 3, 18, 22, 26, 28, 42, 110, 116–7, 134, 171, 180
State, 18, 32, 42, 52, 56, 69, 98, 100, 133, 157, 162, 174, 181, 208
subject/subjectivity, 6, 10, 16, 79, 91, 116, 142–55, 199,

223

210; singular, 6, 103, 115; Western, 3, 6, 13–14, 121–41; women's, 2, 14, 95, 117, 121–41, 142–55
subjective, 10, 15, 92–3, 112, 171, 178, 180, 182, 187
supranational, 61–2, 92, 158, 162, 168, 176
survive/survival, 4, 50, 158

technology, 3, 37, 144, 148, 159, 163, 169–70, 173
thou, 114, 116, 128, 135, 138, 140
tradition, 2, 7, 9–11, 19, 27, 41, 47, 68, 73, 115, 123, 127, 154, 161, 163, 208; women's, 1
transcendence, 47, 116, 138–9
Treaty of Maastricht, 61–2, 73–4, 85, 186, 194, 196, 199, 203, 206–9, 214; of Rome, 202–3
two, ix, 6, 15–16, 22, 26–7, 38, 42, 47, 60, 76, 90, 103, 108–9, 112, 114–8, 121–41, 142–55, 170, 172–3, 180, 182

unconscious, 51, 156
undifferentiated, 37, 66, 124, 131
unemployment, 4, 65, 145
universal/universality, 2, 3, 6, 9–10, 15, 26, 28–9, 37–8, 64, 129, 150, 168, 173, 183, 199

Veil, Simone, 31
violence, 8, 31, 84, 89, 97, 99, 111, 155, 182, 193; sexual, 44, 180–1

woman/women, viii, 1, 4, 6–7, 10–14, 16–17, 22–7, 29, 30, 33, 35–9, 42–3, 55–7, 63, 66, 71, 77, 84, 101, 103, 118, 152–61; Movement, 33, 101, 119
work, 43–4, 55, 57, 60, 75, 82, 89, 103, 132, 142–55, 157–8, 167, 188, 196, 199, 213

young, 17, 55, 59, 65, 67, 70, 77, 106, 119, 173, 213

ATHLONE CONTEMPORARY EUROPEAN THINKERS

Aesthetic Theory
Adorno
0 485 30069 9 HB
0 485 30090 7 PB

Composing for the Films
Adorno & Eisler
0 485 11454 2 HB
0 485 12017 7 PB

Freud and Nietzsche
Assoun
0 485 11483 6 HB

Criticism and Truth
Barthes
0 485 12144 1 PB

Sollers Writer
Barthes
0 485 11337 6 HB

On Nietzsche
Bataille
0 485 30068 0 HB

Nietzsche: The Body and Culture
Blondel
0 485 11391 0 HB

Death: An Essay on Finitude
Dastur
0 485 11487 HB

Telling Time: Sketch of a Phenomenological Chronology
Dastur
0 485 11520 4 HB

Proust and Signs
Deleuze
0 485 12141 7 PB

Kants Critical Philosophy
Deleuze
0 485 12101 8 PB

Difference and Repetition
Deleuze
0 485 11360 0 HB
0 485 12102 6 PB

The Fold: Leibniz and the Baroque
Deleuze
0 485 11421 6 HB
0 485 12087 9 PB

Anti-Oedipus: Capitalism and Schizophrenia
Deleuze & Guattari
Preface by Michel Foucault
0 485 30018 4 PB

A Thousand Plateaus
Deleuze & Guattari
0 485 11335 X HB
0 485 12058 4 PB

Cinema 1: The Movement-Image
Deleuze
0 485 12081 X PB

Cinema 2: The Time-Image
Deleuze
0 485 11359 7 HB
0 485 12070 4 PB

Dialogues
Deleuze & Parnet
0 485 11333 3 HB

Foucault
Deleuze
0 485 12154 9 PB

Logic of Sense
Deleuze
0 485 30063 X HB

Nietzsche and Philosophy
Deleuze
0 485 12053 4 PB

Dissemination
Derrida
0 485 12093 3 PB

Positions
Derrida
0 485 30000 1 HB
0 485 12055 0 PB

The Memory of Thought: On Heidegger and Adorno
Düttmann
0 485 11489 5 HB

The Gift of Language: Memory and Promise in Adorno, Benjamin, Heidegger and Rosenzweig
Düttmann
0 485 11488 7 HB
0 485 12161 1 PB

Nietzsche's Philosophy
Fink
0 485 11484 4 HB

Death and the Labyrinth: The World of Raymond Roussel
Foucault
0 485 11336 8 HB
0 485 12059 3 PB

The Three Ecologies
Guattari
0 485 11555 7 HB

pleroma – Reading in Hegel
Hamacher
0 485 11457 7 HB

Towards the Definition of Philosophy
Heidegger
0 485 11508 5 HB

The Nature of Truth
Heidegger
0 485 11509 3 HB

On the Essence of Human Freedom
Heidegger
0 485 11516 6 HB

Phenomenology of Intuition and Expression
Heidegger
0 485 11415 8 HB

To Speak is Never Neutral
Irigaray
0 485 11452 9 HB
0 485 12089 5 PB

Democracy Begins Between Two
Irigaray
0 485 11503 4 HB
0 485 12123 9 PB

To Be Two
Irigaray
0 485 11492 5 HB
0 485 12120 4 PB

The Forgetting of Air
Irigaray
0 485 11491 7 HB
0 485 12119 0 PB

Elemental Passions
Irigaray
0 485 11409 7 HB
0 485 12079 8 PB

An Ethics of Sexual Difference
Irigaray
0 485 30067 2 HB
0 485 30070 2 PB

Nietzsche and the Vicious Circle
Klossowski
0 485 11440 2 HB

Explosion I
Kofman
0 485 11458 5 HB

Explosion II
Kofman
0 485 11459 3 HB

Camera Obscura: of Ideology
Kofman
0 485 11490 9 HB

Socrates: Fictions of a Philosopher
Kofman
0 485 11460 7 HB

Nietzsche and Metaphor
Kofman
0 485 11422 4 HB
0 485 12098 4 PB

The Philosophical Imaginary
Le Doeuff
0 485 11352 X HB

Everyday Life in the Modern World
Lefebvre
0485 30094 X PB

Alterity & Transcendence
Levinas
0 485 11519 0 HB
0 485 12152 2 PB

Entre Nous: Essays on Thinking-of-the-Other
Levinas
0 485 11465 8 HB

Proper Names
Levinas
0 485 11466 6 HB

In the Time of the Nations
Levinas
0 485 11449 6 HB

Beyond the Verse
Levinas
0 485 11430 5 HB

Outside the Subject
Levinas
0 485 11412 7 HB
0 485 12097 6 PB

Difficult Freedom: Essays on Judaism
Levinas
0 485 11379 1 HB

Redemption and Utopia
Löwy
0 485 11406 2 HB

Sex and Existence: Simone de Beauvoir's *The Second Sex*
Lundgren-Gothlin
Preface by Toril Moi
0 485 11469 0 HB
0 485 12124 7 PB

Libidinal Economy
Lyotard
0 485 12083 6 PB

Deconstruction and the 'Unfinished Project of Modernity'
Norris
0 485 11564 6 HB
0 485 12159 X PB

The Conflict of Interpretations: Essays in Hermeneutics I
Ricoeur
0 485 30061 3 HB

From Text to Action: Essays in Hermeneutics II
Ricouer
0 485 30064 8 PB

Hegel: Contra Sociology
Rose
0 485 12036 4 PB

Nietzsche: An Introduction
Vattimo
0 485 11485 2 HB
0 485 12118 2 PB